R. Schenk
103 R. Mulberry
San Antonio, TX 78212
(210) 733-0019

HOME DOG

Revolutionary
Rapid
Training
Method

HOME DOG

How to Train
Your Dog to Obey
and Protect You

**RICHARD A.
WOLTERS**

Author of *Family
Dog, Game Dog,* and
Water Dog

Illustrated with Photographs
by the Author

Foreword by Gene Hill
Associate Editor, *Field & Stream*

Dutton
New York

DUTTON
Published by the Penguin Group
Penguin Books USA Inc., 375 Hudson Street,
New York, New York 10014, U.S.A.
Penguin Books Ltd, 27 Wrights Lane,
London W8 5TZ, England
Penguin Books Australia Ltd, Ringwood,
Victoria, Australia
Penguin Books Canada Ltd, 10 Alcorn Avenue,
Toronto, Ontario, Canada M4V 3B2
Penguin Books (N.Z.) Ltd, 182-190 Wairau Road,
Auckland 10, New Zealand

Penguin Books Ltd, Registered Offices:
Harmondsworth, Middlesex, England

*First published by Dutton, an imprint of Dutton Signet, a division of Penguin Books USA
Inc. This is a revised edition of the book formerly titled* City Dog.
Distributed in Canada by McClelland & Stewart Inc.

14   13   12   11   10   9   8   7   6

Library of Congress Catalog Card Number: 84-70034

Printed in the United States of America
Designed by Richard A. Wolters

Dedicated to making our dogs better citizens.

CONTENTS

FOREWORD

Gene Hill
Associate Editor, *Field & Stream*

If you've often thought about having a dog around your home and have been discouraged by remembering all the dogs you've seen that misbehave, jump all over people, and seem more parasite than pet, I don't blame you. But that's the fault of the people—not the dog.

A dog isn't automatically a good companion or a protective friend who barks at strangers. You both have to make a few adjustments to each other, starting from the first "hello." Fortunately, as you'll see just by glancing through this book, none of this is difficult. In fact it's fun for the both of you.

As there are all sorts of dogs and all sorts of dog books—some are right for you and some aren't. This one covers a few details that I doubt you'll find anywhere else. No doubt you have some idea of what kind of a dog you'd like: small, or large and intimidating; curly and cute, or sporting or stylish. That doesn't matter as much as *which* dog—the individual itself you pick, and here Dick Wolters offers a very scientific test that's proved to be as accurate and as close to foolproof as anything I know.

Almost any dog will end up being a comfort—most of the time. But with Dick's simple-to-follow and easy-to-understand method you'll very quickly find a friend that will do a lot more for you than lick the back of your hand. We don't often enough think of a home dog as being really functional and practical. But in these times, why not, if it's part of a dog's nature that can easily be brought out? It's instinctive in most dogs to be protective of its owner and family. All you have to do to produce an alarm dog is reinforce the trait that is already there, as Wolters shows you how to do with a simple routine of short training sessions. The results will amaze you.

I have a unique advantage over most writers of forewords. I've trained dogs with Dick and using his methods. I've met people all over the country who have told me how pleased they've been with the results they've had using Wolters's rapid and simple approach to dog control. You might say that I'm a good authority on Dick's authority; I know what I'm saying is valid—or I simply wouldn't be doing it. I very much agree that a dog is one of man's most delightful friends—*if* it's trained. And I also know from my own experience that a dog loves training and delights in doing the things that please its owner. This is a positive world, and we all want approbation for being good at our jobs—a dog is not one whit different.

This is a very simple book. Easy to read and illustrated with great care and exactness. Why? Because Dick Wolters has written over half a dozen dog books and even *he's* learned something by repetition! I advise you to follow the book as exactly as you can, because the simplicity is deceptive. There is a vast depth of scientific know-how couched in these instructions. Unlike most dog-training books where the author tells you how good he is, this one tells you, and rightly, how good both you and your dog can be.

I can't imagine living without a dog. Dogs are woven deeply into my life pattern. I know I would be less of a person without them. That's the only thing that I can add to this book: to remind you that when the relationship is complete, you'll be the one who looks eagerly to coming home, being taken for a walk, and doing the little things that will make your dog say "I love you." Your life will never again be the same and I promise you won't want it any other way.

HOME DOG

1. IN THE BEGINNING

Home dog? In sheer numbers the dog has been the most successful beast in the animal kingdom, not only in reaching our hearts but in coming to live under our very roofs almost as one of us. In so many ways it has been like bringing another child into our home. Many of our dogs have been bred, traditionally, for specific work. In today's society, that work is often forgotten, not only by man but by the dog himself. Dogs play a new role in our homes, and like our children, they too need an education for living in this small social group. Hence this book.

The home is going through dramatic social changes, but it is still the core of our society, and it is not very strange to find man's best friend right there with us.

Possibly because of the changes in our homes today, more and more people need the companionship and affection the dog gives so freely, and many want dogs for the added protection they can offer. The situation isn't much different from what it was thousands of years ago when man and dog lived together in a cave—apartments today aren't much different from holes in a cliff. As man learned to build better and better homes, as his own civilization progressed, the dog went right along with him. Dogs have been willing to adapt to man's way of living wherever and however he chose to make his home.

Dogs come in all shapes and sizes. Some are fancy and some are just mutts, but they are increasing in numbers. For some people this is a blessing and for others it's a cause for concern. More and more our life-style is physically close and emotionally distant. Because we are physically close to one another, the dog owner has to take full responsibility toward others for his or her four-legged charge. An unruly dog can cause problems with one's neighbors. Because we live today at a "distance" from others emotionally, the dog has resumed the role he played when man and dog first became friends aeons ago.

In primitive folks tales there are many versions of how man and dog became inseparable friends, but they all add up to the same thing. In the beginning—and for this version it doesn't matter where it was, except that it was out in the open under the stars—men lived huddled around a fire scared to death that some enemy was about to devour them. Making a living back in that era must have been rather tough going. Small bands of parents and children, aunts and uncles and cousins roamed around hunting for game. Economics worked very simply: by suppertime, either man had his meal or he was some other animal's meal. It was a question of who gobbled whom first. It was a great big tough world in those days, but I wonder if it's much better in our cities today. The big difference was that at that time there were a lot of different kinds of animals, and some didn't make it. Man and dog did make it, but I'm not sure man would have made it without the dog.

There was man, huddled around the fire at night, and a good distance from the fire sat another band of parents and offspring, aunts and uncles and cousins. They had four legs and a tail. They ate and barked. They were pretty smart. They had their economics all figured out, too. They let man do most of the work each day, and then, when he cooked his meal at the fire, they started to bark and yip. Of course, this was all before the days of Pepto-Bismol, and who could enjoy the roast leg of woolly mammoth or shaggy horse with all that racket going on? To quiet down his neighbors, man threw the supper bones at him, and that was the economics of the dog world. The loudest barker got the most food heaved at him. Is it possible that we can credit the dog with teaching man about ecology—about how to keep the campsite clean?

When man ran into a shortage and there wasn't even a crown rib to eat, he learned an important lesson. When he had no garbage to throw at the dogs, they left, since they weren't interested in eating stones. Without the yipping dogs around at night, man soon discovered that he couldn't sleep. The dogs had better ears and would give a warning when danger approached out of the dark. Without the dogs around, man became afraid that he wouldn't hear some big ferocious thing steal into camp and carry off one of his wives. God forbid! The upshot of all this was that after many sleepless nights, he invited the dogs to join his household for dinner, and they stayed for thousands of years.

When the two kinds of families started living together, man soon discovered that his new friend was very helpful in hunting. They both had a good thing going.

Those early dogs must have been pretty smart, but I wonder why they ever stuck with man. If I'd been around in those early prehistoric days, I never would have bet that man would survive or actually end up at the top of the heap in the animal kingdom. Early man just didn't seem to have what it took to survive; he wasn't designed very well. He wasn't the swiftest, the biggest, or the strongest. His skin was soft and didn't protect him from the elements, let alone from being punctured by an enemy. He had only a fist for fighting, nothing for stinging, and not even a claw or hoof to swing. His fingernails were only good for chewing when he was scared, and his bite wasn't even as good as that of a Pekingese. If he had evolved with better senses of hearing and smelling, and had longer legs so he could run faster, man might not have needed dogs to help him survive. They might have ended up today in our city zoos instead of in our bedrooms.

Back in the era of Adam and Eve, the man/dog relationship was truly the real beginning of a love affair and mutual aid society. It has lasted for thousands of generations. Man—that is, the male—seemed to think that he had the best part of the bargain and that he owned the dog and Eve. On the surface it appears as though he did own the dog. The dog hunted for him, herded livestock, fished by swimming the net lines across estuaries, transported him and his belongings by cart and sled, and was on sentry duty twenty-four hours a day. Through all this time, Adam, with Eve and the dog, made great advancements and built gigantic cities—and what has happened? Adam has been outwitted by both Eve and his friend the dog. Eve now has Women's Lib, and the dog, untrained, just doesn't work at all. How many city dogs hunt? Do any herd livestock? None swim the net lines. When it comes to travel, they are more of a pain in the neck than a help, and as sentries, most of them would lick the face of a burglar and beg for a handout instead of scaring the intruder off.

Yet, in spite of everything, more and more dogs are being brought to the cities. This is an unusual trend.

In the past, when man didn't need the services of an animal he had domesticated, he banished it. When was the last time you saw an ox walking down the street? Within our lifetime the workhorse has been given the heave-ho. Not so the dog. Quite the reverse. The dog gets put on social security at birth. Unless he's used for protection, he gets unemployment compensation and medical care for free. Whereas man is willing to work until he is sixty-five for these benefits, the dog gets them by sleeping in the master's chair all day, resting up for his five minutes of work, which consists of wagging his tail and jumping around a bit to greet the boss when he drags his tail home from the office. Who owns whom? Which one is the dumb animal?

Maybe man is not as stupid as I have made him out. Today, man needs the dog mainly as a friend and protector. Human progress has led to an increasingly urbanized society. Most of the hunting these days is done in a supermarket, searching for food at prices the family can afford.

New problems have arisen. In today's society, people are splintered into their own little groups. You would think that with people living so close together in cities, they would have lots of friends and many social outlets. But it hasn't worked that way. Neighbors in an apartment house don't even know each other's names. Urban living produces suspicion and a calloused society where there is little respect for the individual. Loneliness abounds within concrete walls. The dog's devotion to man is a needed ingredient in the life style man has created for himself.

For many people, a dog is the only source of comfort and affection. If you take a walk into New York City's Central Park, you'll see men and women of all ages, a cross section of our society, walking dogs. A basic need in man is to feel

Dogs, crowded even in New York City's Central Park, must be peaceable citizens.

wanted, and the dog satisfies that need for his master. The basic need in the dog is to play the role of a friend, and he doesn't care whether his master is black, yellow, or white, whether he lives downtown or uptown.

Another reason why more and more people are keeping dogs, and big ones at that, is for the sense of security dogs provide. A mugger isn't going to know whether or not a dog will protect his master. Instead of taking the chance, he'll seek out another victim. We'll show you how to make your dog into a protector without making him dangerous. He'll become an alarm dog. He'll give the alarm on command by barking when you feel the situation warrants its.

There is one respect in which the dog has an advantage over his friend: dogs seem to adapt to new things more easily than men. Didn't men kill Socrates because he had new ideas? Wasn't the discoverer of anesthesia practically ridden out of Boston on a rail? And didn't they laugh at the Wright brothers? The resistance men have put up to new ideas on raising a dog is but one example of how hard it is for us to break with tradition. For a dozen or more years animal behaviorists have been telling us that their studies of dogs indicated some rather startling facts about our old friends. These scientists have come up with a new dog training method; simply stated, it's an early training method.

Ever since the early sixteenth century, when the first dog training book was written, the theory was that dogs should not be trained until they are physically mature, about six months old. The new scientific information proves this to be wrong. Using this material, I've produced three books for the hunter written in English so simple that even my dogs can understand it.* It took time for the new training method to catch on, but now tens of thousands of hunters have used it successfully. At first, and for some time, the traditionalists scoffed, but dogs trained for work have proven the success of the method.

It's simple enough: scientists have shown that dogs with early training do much better than those that don't go to school until they are almost full grown. Would you believe that a dog makes his strongest bond with man between seven and twelve weeks of age, and if you start this love affair at a later time the bond will never be as strong as it could have been? We'll tell you all about that; and there will be some new thinking, also, for the professional dog raiser who finds this kind of knowledge bad for business.

Don't argue with *me* about this early training method. You'll have to direct your skepticism to the scientists, and you'll lose your arguments—they've got the proof. With an early training method we're going to mold the dog to your needs and train him in such a way that he won't realize he's being trained. He won't learn bad habits because he won't know any other way of doing things. (Don't you wish we could do this with our kids?)

Now that I have promised you a hint that we will have a new program for the training of your dog, the question is, why a book on the Home Dog? Well, an unruly dog in the close quarters forced on us in many communities can be such a headache for you as to outweigh the love and companionship he'll give you. A dog may not be able to understand the Golden Rule, but his behavior should make it seem as though he did. A noisy dog isn't going to be loved by your neighbors, and, since he's yours, you'll come under fire. Sharing a crowded elevator with a high-strung dog isn't a very pleasant experience for the very young or the elderly. Messy sidewalks aren't pleasant for anyone. Even the overfriendly dog is a pain in the neck. The vicious dog is another problem altogether and should be banned completely. We'll address ourselves to these problems, and we'll also show you how to train a dog to be a new kind of security guard—a safe one to have around.

In our society, we all, men and dogs, have to be good citizens to make it work. Theoretically, that's what education is all about. A well-trained dog, just like a well-trained person, is a pleasure to deal with, especially in our high-strung, up-tight city life.

So your dog is going to school to become a good citizen, and you're going to school yourself to be his teacher. The starting point is to figure out what your dog's job is going to be. Then we'll show you what courses you are going to teach. But first, and most important, you will want to select the best pupil for the job to be done.

* *Gun Dog, Water Dog,* and *Game Dog* (E. P. Dutton, Inc.)

2. SELECTING THE HOME DOG

Dogs come in all shapes and sizes . . . just like people. They have all kinds of hair, they wear it long, short, frowzy, straight, curly or even in a pompadour. Along the way some place, someone suggested that all the big dogs should live in the country and that the small ones were best for the city. A city slicker doesn't pick a husband or wife by size—by shape, yes; but he or she doesn't suppose that a tall spouse would feel confined in the close quarters of a city apartment. Why should it be any different for dogs? A good dog, like a good spouse, will adapt to any reasonable living conditions if there is a little love and affection in the living. As far as dogs are concerned, a lot can be said in favor of many of the larger breeds. They are not as feisty and high-strung as their smaller cousins. The amateur trainer seems to have a lot more success training the larger breeds. Of course, this should not be carried too far. If you drive a Volkswagen and will be transporting your dog, you might have some problems if you pick a Great Dane. Beagles are nice small dogs, only about fifteen inches high. If you consider their heredity, they should be on rabbit trails in the woods and not on leashes following mink coats down Main Street. But even they can be happy in the city. The point is that this old wives' tale about size is just a myth. Big dogs can be healthy and happy in the home, and with our serious concern these days with law and order, the big dog is much desired.

There is an old saying among dog people, "If you can pick out a spouse, you should be able to pick out a dog." I'm not sure it's that simple. You need a lot of luck picking out a wife or a husband. We should be able to be more objective when it comes to the dog.

CHOOSING A BREED

There are almost 120 different breeds that are recognized by the American Kennel Club. That's a long list to choose from, and it includes some strange four-leggers. These are the purebreds, and their pedigrees are most likely better than your in-laws'!

This chapter will give you some general advice about selecting the breed and then some new information about picking the particular dog out of the litter.

Don't choose a dog because you've seen the breed in a television soap opera. Lassie has done more to ruin a good breed of dog than you can imagine. Everybody falls in love with the beauty and human quality that are portrayed, and as a result, breeders get more calls for the dog than they can fill. Soon a high-strung strain of the breed is in households all over the country, and this can only lead to problems for the amateur trainer.

Don't pick one of the most popular breeds. Every month the AKC puts out a list of the number of dog registrations. The dogs are broken down into their groups. In the sporting group, the dog that is way out in front, with not even a close second, is the Irish setter. True, he's one of the handsomest dogs on the whole list. He's been bred for his beauty, and as a result he's not worth the price of dog food to a hunter. His pointing instinct has been neglected and replaced by his fine red coat. That might be all right for those not interested in hunting, but in making the transformation, he's also become the highest strung big dog in the whole AKC listing. He's too excitable for the home.

In the hound group, beagles and dachshunds are currently at the top of the popularity list. Most beagles in this country are still bred for working, so they are good dogs with excellent qualities; but the close second, the dachshund, is a cute, stubborn little devil. He's hard to train and may never become housebroken.

In the working group, the German shepherd heads the list, with the Doberman pinscher second. Neither of these dogs is too trustworthy. There seems to be a myth about the shepherd and the pinscher, that each has two strains, one vicious and one gentle. If it is so, you just try to figure out which one you have when you're buying a puppy. It's easy to understand these days why the Doberman and the shepherd are being overproduced. With crime as rampant as it is on our city streets, the public is turning to these dogs for a sense of security. They "say" trouble to the stranger, but they can also be trouble for the owner and his family. Things will only get worse because the demand is still growing. Incidentally, the collie, near the top of this list and now a nervous breed, is nowhere near as smart as the Border collie, a dog not recognized by the AKC. Another point: most of the Seeing-Eye German shepherds are bred by the Seeing-Eye people themselves. They will not accept outside bred dogs for their training because they can't be sure any longer what they will get.

Near the bottom of that working group list is a dog that is getting much attention from trainers—the Bouviers des Flandres. He's smart, great with kids, and yet can be trained as an attack dog.

The terrier group is made up of a bunch of tough little dogs. The miniature schnauzer is the most popular of them, and rightly so: he's a fine little dog and is the exception to my theory that it's best to avoid the most popular breed in a group.

In the toy group, it's the Pekingese that wins the popularity contest. It's hard to understand, but I've got some friends whose choice of mates I could never understand either. Way down that list is the pug, in my view a much more likable dog.

The poodle, in the nonsporting group, is the overall winner in the dog world. This is again an example of overbreeding. In my book, the only poodle that is worth his salt any more is the standard. The toy and miniature have been bred for a fancy market, but the standard has remained the smart king that he is.

Besides the fact that a popularity contest is not the way to choose your dog, there is another point to be made here. If you are buying a dog and the breeder shows enthusiasm over the fact that a pooch's bloodlines are some of the best stock in the country, don't consider that as a point in the dog's favor unless you are going to show him. The dumb blonde jokes have been around a long time, and they aren't so far different from the stories about show dogs. Breeding for conformation alone isn't my idea of the best thing for either the dog or the public. Some day when the dog show people make it mandatory for a dog to have its full obedience training before it can enter a show, I might get interested in the "sport" of dog shows.

GOOD FOR CHILDREN

American water spaniel	English setter	Labrador retriever
basset hound	English shepherd	old English sheep dog
beagle	foxhound	pointer
boxer	golden retriever	poodle (standard)
Brittany spaniel	Great Dane	Saint Bernard
bull dog	Irish water spaniel	springer spaniel
coonhound		

NOT GOOD FOR CHILDREN

American cocker spaniel	husky	Pekingese
American toy fox terrier	Italian greyhound	Pomeranian
Chesapeake Bay retriever	Japanese spaniel	Samoyed
Chihuahua	Kerry blue terrier	Scotch terrier
chow	malemute	spitz
dachshund	Maltese terrier	toy Manchester
Doberman pinscher	Mexican hairless	wire-haired fox terrier
German shepherd	miniature pinscher	Yorkshire terrier

It was some years ago that I published a list of the breeds that were, for one reason or another, good and bad for children. This list was compiled by one of the biggest humane dog organizations in New York. The listings were made by keeping a record of the placements in homes of the different breeds. After a period of time each owner was asked about his dog and how it was making out. The list is not complete. Some dogs were not included because the sampling was too small, and some breeds were not tested. That published list caused a lot of grief because the individual breeders wanted my scalp if the dogs they handled were in the bad column. A dog's temperament wasn't the only criterion. Some breeds made the bad list because they required too much care or didn't take to training easily. Be that as it may, here is the list again, with a few modifications.

There is an old theory that man creates his dog in his own image. Through selective breeding, people in an area develop the type of dog that fits their personality. It seems to be true. Mid-European or German dogs are one-man, hard-headed animals who need a firm hand in training. These "Prussian" dogs are very different from English dogs. Like their owners, English dogs tend to have a quiet dignity and to be good natured.

Most of us, when faced with making a decision, have a preconceived idea of what we want or don't want (for example, the lady who didn't like the hunting breeds because she felt it was impolite to point). If you have no idea of what dog you want, it may help to step in front of a mirror and think about it. If you are a big guy and decide on a Pomeranian, one or the other of you is going to look rather foolish walking down the street.

One of the questions often asked is whether a purebred dog is better than the more democratic "57 Variety" mutt. If style is important to you, the fact that your dog has a pedigree may add pleasure for you, but it won't mean a thing to the dog. Those papers will have nothing to do with his intelligence. The only thing they do mean is that you will know approximately what the pooch is going to look like when he grows up. All puppies are cute, cuddly fluffballs, but remember that some will grow to weigh 6 pounds and some will make it to 160.

If there are young children in the household, adding a dog is going to be a big event. Don't fall into the trap of letting the children make the decision as to what breed you are going to live with for the next fifteen years. They'll learn to love the dog of your choice. The children shouldn't even go to the kennel to pick out the particular dog. This job is for adults, and we will have a lot to say about it.

SEX . . . THERE'S A DIFFERENCE

Male vs. Female. An age-old question. Which is better? There's a feeling among dog people that the female makes the best pet. She is less likely to roam and therefore seems more affectionate. Males can be just as loving; it has a lot to do with the way they are brought up. Some males will be difficult to handle and will want to show their dominance, but we will show you how to steer clear of such a dog. It's quite true that females are less likely to fight. They're the smaller members of the breed, and the general opinion is that they're easier to housebreak. It's not necessarily true that they're less rambunctious, but many dog people think they are. Many feel that the female will understand your moods better—just female intuition, I guess.

Facts About the Female. The only time that the female attracts the males is when she's in season. A bitch's first heat occurs at approximately nine months of age, then in most cases she goes on a six-month cycle. The heat lasts about twenty-one days. She'll attract males during this time, but she'll only stand for a dog about five days in the middle of the heat. An old English poacher's trick on nightly hunting expeditions was to take along a bitch in season. This was to lure the gamekeeper's watchdog from his post. Because the male can be diverted from his job, some folks feel a female is a more reliable dog.

WHERE TO LOOK

Where do you get a dog? Most of the experts say to steer away from the pet stores, claiming that they sell a dog as if it were a piece of beef and have to move their stock over the counter as fast as possible. Like everything else, there are good pet dealers and bad ones. However, the professional breeder's kennel is the place to get a registered dog if you expect to show it in the ring. If he's a good breeder, he's going to stand behind his product. So try to get a line on the dealer; you'd do the same thing if you were buying an automobile. Ask him for the names of some of the people who have bought pups from him. You want recent sales, not old friends. Call the parties and ask how they like their pups and the dealer. Of course, when you go out to see the place you will learn a lot by observing whether it is clean—whether the kennel has a fresh odor—and by noting the condition of the other adult dogs. If the place looks like a dog factory, steer clear. Many vets suggest buying dogs from breeders in less populated areas. Overproduction leads to problems.

PICKING THE PUPPY FROM THE LITTER

When you have decided on the breed and the kennel from which to buy the pup, the next step is the most important . . . choosing the one dog that's going to be yours. Any sale should be contingent on your vet's seeing the pup, but here are some things to look for yourself. Are the pup's eyes clear? A discharge can spell real trouble. A heavy discharge from the nose is also serious; it can mean distemper, the major killer of dogs. Examine for signs of diarrhea. Run your hand through the pup's hair. His skin should be soft and pliable and have a good gloss, and he should be free of parasites. Watch the pup move around. Is he agile? If so, the chances are he has no nutritional deficiencies. Turn the pup over and check his navel. A lump means an umbilical hernia, which can mean later trouble. Play with him and check his teeth. A brown stain is a sign that he has had distemper. His gums should be pink and clear, and his teeth should be regular and form a good bite. If not, he will have trouble digesting his food.

If you are smart, you will make more than one visit to the kennel before you buy the pup. If they all look alike, paint nail polish on the ones you are interested in so you can be sure which they were when you come to observe again. Ask to see the mother, and you'll get a good idea of what your dog is going to look like. Her condition can tell you much about how the breeder handles his dogs.

Be sure to get the complete papers and record on the pup you select. It will be important to your vet to know what shots he has had, and it'll be important to you to get the feeding instructions.

A NEW WAY OF SELECTING THE PUP FROM THE LITTER

There are a lot of old wives' tales about raising puppies and children. There are certainly a lot of messed-up people in our modern society, and that also goes for dogs. We will try to show you how to make the best start possible. There is no sense starting with two strikes against you, and the information we'll give you is based on scientific fact, not conjecture.

As you read the following section, you will find some startling information on the mental development of the young dog. We have already said that the strongest bond between man and dog is made before the dog is twelve weeks old. This will be explained in depth as you read on. For now we will refer to that only to say that we will give the information on selecting a puppy, not a full-grown or even a half-grown dog. This may seem cruel, because what I am saying is that you are not to give a dog a home unless you start with that dog from the very best time. That best time, for you and your dog, is the forty-ninth day of the pup's life. This, as you will see, is not an arbitrary rule; it's a proven date.

There will be plenty of people who will not read this book and will not use the information given here. For many reasons, they will give homes to the older dogs who need them. I have no ax to grind. I do not sell dogs nor do I have any association with any organization that places dogs into homes. I can only give the facts to you, the reader, as I see them, and that is why you buy such a book at this. Some people would rather get a dog that has been housebroken so they won't have the mess and the trouble. Some people are afraid to handle a very small puppy because they think they might not do a good job of training. Whatever your reason, let me try to convince you that you must start with a seven-week-old pup. If you disagree, you'll be missing most of the thrust of this book.

Most pups are picked from the litter through love at first sight. It's usually the aggressive one that wins out. He could grow to be the most difficult to train. Now we have a better way to pick the pup . . . by testing.

You may ask, how can one go to see a litter of pups and make any real judgments? They are all so cute and friendly. Even as you watch them, one is going to win your heart because of a funny spot he has or the way he plays with your hand. Of course, we'll assume that you have examined each for physical problems and that they are all in good shape.

Just to stay away from the listless, shy, or nervous pups is not enough. To make the decision on which one in the litter is to be yours, you now have to know what temperament is going to be best for your needs. When you sit on the ground in the middle of a litter, the puppy that flails about and bites at your hand when you go to pick him up may seem cute, but when he grows up he may not be suited for a family with small children or for an elderly person. The pup that becomes quiet and comfortable when you pick him up will probably accept the rough play that children display with puppies, and senior citizens will enjoy his gentle, submissive behavior. Such a pup will take to training readily. Unfortunately, too many people seek out the bold dogs, the ones that stride through the litter so that all the other pups make way for them. Many of these dogs end up at the humane society shelter because they couldn't get along with the kids or the older persons in a family.

The six-week-old pup that displays a high degree of social independence in his litter and that spurns praise and petting will be a tough dog to train. He's the kind who, among other dogs, must keep proving his dominance. He becomes the scrapper and just the kind of dog that is killed by a car while chasing a stray canine that has come into his territory. This doesn't mean, of course, that he is necessarily a neurotic dog. All litters have their bullies and their wallflowers. The bully often won't respond favorably to scolding, and in the wrong home environment he can be a problem because he still wants to be the pack leader. But in the right home, with a strong master, this dog could be a fine pet. The opposite case can be made for the wallflower of the litter.

We don't want to give the impression that all bullies, or for that matter all wallflowers, become behavioral problems, but there is a potential difficulty here that can be avoided. It is indeed a rare but fortunate puppy buyer who finds a breeder who will fit the puppy to the environment he will be going into. Most dogs are sold by letting the pups work their magic charm on the buyers . . . it's love at first sight.

In my book *Game Dog*, which deals with the hunting retrievers, I have discussed ways of observing a litter of puppies that the average person can use to take a lot of the guesswork and luck out of the puppy selection. What our observation of the litter is supposed to do is reveal the behavior tendencies of each pup. This is important because you should realize that the pup you choose now will grow to be the dog you will live with for many years. You may need the cooperation of the breeder to take the time to make this selection.

Actually the breeder should not object; there is no need to sell a Ferrari to a little old lady.

We shall be using a modified version of the Campbell procedure, a Puppy Behavior Test* to try to find out where individual pups stand in their litter's pecking order. We shall explain why the change in the test is being recommended and show how we shall use the modified version.

The purpose of the testing? We recognize that all litters develop their own pecking order...from the dominant pup to the submissive one, and all the ones in between. For our purpose the individual personalities, such as the dominant and the shy, have to be identified. As you will see, the first step, for the average dog owner, in selecting will be to eliminate these two at the extremes of the pecking order. By the seventh week the pattern of the order is well established.

But before taking up this procedure in detail, I should note that it cannot be expected to work in every case. Other methods of pup evaluation have also been devised, though the best of them may be too technical for the average buyer. Recent information has modified the views of many scientists and breeders about puppy testing.

Dr. Michael W. Fox, one of our leading animal behaviorists, approaches the selection problem entirely differently than is done in the Campbell procedure. In Fox's book *The Dog: Its Domestication and Behavior* is a chapter titled, "Heart Rate and Plasma Cortisol as Predictors of Temperament." This is a very technical discussion of the relation between heart rate and temperament. Pups with the highest resting heart rate in the litter seem to be more outgoing, inquisitive, and independent and this continues into maturity. Scientists like Fox are not seeking a "cure-all" test for picking puppies. There is no such thing, according to them. What they seek is a battery of neurological and physiological tests that will reveal the personality pattern of a pup. I just don't see a buyer picking out his pup with a stethoscope.

Because I am not a breeder, I also have to listen to what the breeders are saying. Many have spoken to me, but Jack Jagoda of Southland Kennels in Stafford, Virginia, has expressed it best so I will let him be their spokesman.

"I object," says Jagoda, "to the buyer coming into my kennel armed with a copy of the Campbell Puppy Behavior Test (which seems to be the most popular puppy-selecting method at the moment) and asking my permission to run it. I have deliberately run the test at different times of the day and have gotten different readings on the same pups. It seemed to have a lot to do with the mood of the pups at that time. My observation is that it can't be done in an afternoon. You have to get the whole picture to make this kind of a

---

*The original Campbell procedure was developed by William E. Campbell and appears in his book *Behavior Problems in Dogs* (American Veterinary Publications Inc., Drawer KK, Santa Barbara, California 93102).

decision, and a one-shot test is not going to be accurate, especially when given by people who buy one pup every ten years." Jack and his wife, Diana, use a practical testing system. He says, "We've got our method; we devote many hours of personal contact each day to our pups. We know where each one stands. If the buyers wants to know, we can tell him."

The truth of the matter is that the buyer of a pup is at a disadvantage. The breeders are the ones who could have all the answers if only they took the time and had the knowledge and desire to study their pups closely enough to give the customer the guidance and information he deserves. In some ways buying a pup is like choosing a wife through a marriage broker—there has to be trust someplace.

So far what we have been talking about is a way to identify the aggressive, outgoing, timid, dependent, or passive aspects of the pup; these are all socially oriented qualities. But there is more to the selection of the hunting pup than these social attributes. How do you test for the attributes of a dog? Jagoda marks the Lab litters with a spot of different-colored paint, males on the neck and females on the rump. As they grow week by week, he can keep tabs on what "color" is doing what. He gets to learn which one attacks the food vigorously and which one shies back, how they respond to play and to him. This simple observation gives a quick overview of the social order.

About the fifth or sixth week a game of fetch with a ball is a good way to observe the make-up of the litter. The way they chase will show which one is the bull and the shy one will show up also. The ones that are spunky and play in the game but do not dominate will be in the middle portion of the pecking order. The new trainer will make out best if he takes a pup out of the litter who is in the "middle of the road"—and that is what we shall try to show with this modified Campbell test. We will want a dog who has get-up-and-go but not "charge," a pup who is spunky and not a sissy. We'll steer away from the "wallflower" in the litter, who can be even more of a problem than the bull of the litter.

We can go on the assumption that if the pup is a bull at five weeks, he'll most likely be a bull at five years; if he's people-oriented at five weeks, there is a good chance of his being people-oriented at five years; if he's shy and unsure at five weeks, he'll probably be the same at five years. Of course there is no guarantee of this, and that is the weakness Dr. Fox finds with the Campbell test. A dog can be seriously "scarred" or helped in his rearing. The animal behaviorists say the test looks good on paper but has its limitations and should not be considered as gospel.

Jack Volhard, in his book, *Training Your Dog: The Step by Step Manual*, uses and expands on the Campbell procedure. Rutherford and Neil, in their book, *How to Raise a Puppy You Can Live With*, again spell out the Campbell test. I too have used this test in the modified form. It worked for me and it's the only "ball game in town" for the average guy. I feel that the Campbell test has merit, but that the procedure can be made more practical with some modification.

A MODIFIED VERSION OF CAMPBELL'S BEHAVIOR TEST FOR PUPPIES

The test should be run before the litter is seven weeks of age. Each pup should be carried individually to the test area, which should be unfamiliar to the puppy and have nothing to divert his attention. A fenced-in lawn is best. When you take the pup to the test area, say nothing. Just gently carry him in your arms. The carrying should be without incident; we do not want the pup to be upset or excited. There are four parts to the test. You are trying to find the most aggressive and most passive pups as they compare to one another. With Labs and Goldens, don't be surprised if you find out that they test similarly. Run the tests during the time of day when the litter is alert and playful.

He ran off! He's not people-oriented. On the next page see how his littermate did.

Does He Like People?

When you reach the middle of the testing area, set the pup on the ground. Then quickly walk on until you're about ten feet from the pup. Kneel down, get the pup's attention by clapping your hands and gently coax him by voice. You are to observe how quickly and willingly he runs over to join you.

This friendly pup hesitated, then came with a little trepidation, but enjoyed it.

You will be comparing each of the pups, noting whether his tail is wagging or drooping. Is he lively, or hesitant, or does he simply not respond to your invitation? This test indicates the extent to which the pup is attracted to people, or whether he is a shy "loner," and how much self-confidence he has.

This pup stayed where he was put down. The tester waited. The pup decided he wanted no part of this . . . this shy dog wanted to hide . . . not a good pup to take.

Come with Me

Stand close to the pup and then walk off in a casual fashion. As you do so, carefully observe the pup's reaction. How willingly and enthusiastically did he tag along after you? Was his tail up, and was he underfoot? Did he charge you, bite your cuffs, and challenge your progress? Did he follow hesitantly with his tail down, or did he simply refuse to follow you?

The next pup, rambunctious, brash, tagged along with no hesitation. He was . . .

. . . aggressive, chewed trouser cuffs, interfered, and took the role of the leader. This pup will need a strong hand in training.

Lying back and making no effort to resist shows he could be shy . . .

. . . fighting squirming, and struggling show he's headstrong.

Learning Takes Restrictions

Turn the pup over, without being rough, so that he is lying on his back, and with your hand on his chest hold him there until he reacts. Observe his reactions. Does he squirm and fight back, nip at your hand, or growl? Does he resist at first, then give up and settle down? Does he try to lick your hand or does he make no resistance at all? Is he a little bull or a lamb? By the degree to which the pup either resists this treatment or goes along with it, you can judge what his reaction to physical control or discipline is likely to be.

33

This pup couldn't have cared less and he accepted the person as the boss.

This one fought. We're looking for a pup that's middle of the road in temperament.

Who is Going to Be the Boss?

Lift the pup with your palms under his tummy. Hold him with his paws three or four inches off the ground until he reacts. There is little the pup can do. He's either going to accept it or not; in this situation you are the boss. How does he react? Does he struggle, and if so, how vigorously? Does he try to lick your hand, or do nothing? His resistance or lack of it in this situation indicates the extent to which he is willing to recognize you as the boss.

HERE IS WHAT IT ALL ADDS UP TO

To put it all into the simplest terms, we want to eliminate the pups at the extreme ends of the pecking order. You will do best with the "middle" dogs. That's the best dog for the average person. He'll be hardy enough to take the training, will socialize easily, and will be an all-around good choice. The bull will be too aggressive. The passive pup would fold under stress and be too submissive.

The two tests, "Does He Like People?" and "Come With Me," will be good indicators of how easily the pup will socialize with people. The "Learning Takes Restrictions" and "Who Is Going to Be the Boss?" tests will be good indicators of how the pup will take to training.

How should you go about using all this information? I would suggest that you visit the litter and spend as much time as possible watching the pups eat, sleep, play, and then run the test procedure outlined above. After eliminating from the choice what you consider to be the most aggressive and most passive pups, take the remainder, one at a time, off into a field and evaluate how they each play "fetch" with the ball. And then there is a personal factor that has to work into all this. After all, you are not buying a few pounds of hamburger. One of those pups, while playing retrieve, will "win you over." It may be his style, the excitement the game arouses in him, his desire to bring the ball to hand, or his looks—all these factors may figure in.

The next thing you have to consider in all of this is your own personality. If you are a tough, demanding trainer, you should go for a more outgoing pup. If you are in the middle of the road, the dog should be the same—but if you are shy, you should still not take a shy dog. You have to fit yourself into this test to make a good decision.

If you don't believe the test, try it anyway—what do you have to lose? And that is just the point. It can help to spot the dominant and shy dogs . . . any one of the others could make it fine in your home. Of course if one of the main purposes is to have a dog for protection or security, the dominant bull will be the best choice. He will be harder to train but it could be worth it to you.

I guess you already know that socially dogs are not much different from people. I once had a great-uncle Louie who should have been tested. There is usually one scrapper in every litter, and I guess that goes for your family, too.

Possibly the most difficult part of this testing is for you to decide just what you want in your dog. There is no one temperament for the home; you should choose a dog with a temperament that suits your needs for the way you live. We have some friends who live in a brownstone in the heart of Greenwich Village in New York. They are very quiet people and have a very aggressive dog. They say the dog helps them to lead their quiet life . . . no one is about to bother them.

I met one young man who said that he wanted a dog that he could talk to; and there they sat on a park bench, apparently having a fine conversation. At any rate, this test will help match the pup's temperament with the life style of the future owner. An active married couple will have different needs from a retired couple or a family with boisterous children . . . and there will be a pup for each environment.

People and dogs communicate . . . they understand . . . they talk.

RECAP

With this simple test for picking the dog best suited to you according to his temperament, we can reexamine the question of which breed is best for the home. Looking at it from the dog's standpoint, it doesn't really matter. Big dog, little dog, long hair, short hair . . . any one will be healthy and lead a happy life with you if your temperaments match and if you give the dog the correct training at the right time. The big decision here is yours. Do you want a big dog for protection? More and more people think this is a very important factor. There are many to choose from, but to repeat, I'd stay away from the most popular breeds. Can you afford to feed a big dog? With prices of food what they are in our cities, a big dog is like having an extra member of the family at the table each night. There seems to be an old wives' tale about the amount of exercise a big dog needs. A dog, like man, can adapt to the kind of conditions dictated by his life style. The farmer lives a very active life and gets a lot of exercise, but his life expectancy is no greater than that of the businessman who sits behind a desk and gets his exercise only on the weekend. The daily walk and the occasional romp will keep the dog fit and will help you, too.

I'm not suggesting that a Great Dane live with you in a one-room apartment, but if that is what you want, it can work out. Some breeds take a lot of care, and this is just one more duty in a busy life, but once again, if you have the time to get the dog groomed or to do it yourself, then you should have no problem. A short-haired dog won't give you the shedding problem, so this will be a consideration. Will a small dog be under foot in a small house, and will this bother you? Will you have a fenced-in yard to put your dog outside to let off steam? Where will you walk your dog? And will there be a lot of other dogs around?

The methods we discussed on pages 25 to 36 are for determining how the dog will get along with people, but they have nothing to do with how he will get along with other dogs. If this is important in your case, you should observe the dog of your choice while he is living with the whole litter. The dog you picked may do very well with people, but in the dog world he may want to be king of the pack...he will tend to grow to be a fighter. Size seems to have little to do with the desire to fight.

The often-asked question—Which breed is right for me?—might best be answered by strolling through a park on a balmy spring evening. You will find every possible breed of dog there if you wait long enough, just as you will see every color and make of car on Fifth Avenue. People like to have their choice, and as far as I am concerned, no one car is best for all the different needs of people.

For some reason, the poodle is considered a good home dog. I believe it's his dash and style that have given him that reputation. On the other hand, the English setter is usually considered a country dog, possibly because of his heritage, yet an aggressive poodle will be more of a problem than a placid English setter. It all comes back to the temperament of the individual dog, and that is the point I want to stress.

I've tried to show you that there is a lot more to picking the right dog for you than merely deciding on the breed, though breed enters into making this decision. We've already said, for example, that some breeds are currently overproduced, and our advice is to stay away from them. Obviously, your choice of a breed will have a lot to do with your own life style. You should be entitled to your likes and dislikes, but modern life often produces extra strains on us, and if that's true in your case, it's especially important to consider the dog's temperament when making your selection.

The next step is to understand something about the mental development of dogs. Then you'll see how easy it's going to be to train yours.

3. THE PUP'S MENTAL DEVELOPMENT

If all went well with the testing of the litter, you have brought home a dog that is going to fit your environment. The aim of the training is to preserve that desired temperament and develop it further. It's thought that a dog's temperament does not reach stabilized maturity until he is one and a half years old, so the pattern of the puppy's life style should be as consistent as possible throughout this period.

We have new problems in living that cause anxieties and stress for dog as well as man. Intellectually, man can see the reasons for sudden occurrences. A simple example: you're walking a young dog on the street when all of a sudden a siren shrills. You understand that there is an emergency, and the loud noise is the only way the authorities can clear the streets to get to the scene. What does the dog think? For him there is no rhyme or reason for the sudden noise. Or suppose your walk takes you near a subway air vent in the sidewalk. As you pass it, a train rumbles by underground. Possibly the man won't even notice it, but all of a sudden out of the ground comes a loud noise. The dog stops. Multiply that by the thousands of stresses the dog may have to encounter, and is it any wonder we get problem dogs?

We as humans have become overcovetous and overdefensive of our possessions in our modern society; it's no different with the dog. It is instinctive with dogs to mark out their territory and defend it. Our dogs are not living free. This is stress-producing. So is the sex life of the average dog; it's miserable; indeed so far from the natural that it, too, adds to the problem. It is no wonder that under intensive, crowded living conditions animals become suspicious and defensive . . . just like the people. It seems obvious from all this that a bad choice for you would be a half-grown dog that has come from a country setting and been plunked into the city. An elevator would most likely scare the daylights out of the poor animal.

The answer to these problems is twofold. First, for reasons we shall see in a moment, the dog should be started in the unfamiliar environment of his new home at the early age of forty-nine days. One reason we are going to start him so young is so that he will know that automobiles, loud noises, strangers, and such are part of life and will not hurt him. We'll make him secure in his environment. As soon as that takes place, we'll start the training to keep him from utter boredom, which is the cause of many adult dog problems, and to make him a good citizen. Training will be part of his job. He'll be trained to warn of danger, to protect you. He needs a job, even if it's only learning tricks, for his own sense of self-importance . . . he's no different from you.

Self-confidence can be just as necessary for the trainer as for the dog. Learning to retrieve the stuffed teddy bear is the job at hand. The pup will soon get the idea and bring it all the way back with a little coaxing. Once learned, retrieving is a fun job.

For centuries, dogs have been trained under the theory that a one-year-old dog can be compared to a seven-year-old child; a two-year-old dog has been likened to a fourteen-year-old adolescent; and at seven years of age the dog was thought to be like a man about to turn the half-century mark. We now know that this seven-to-one ratio is only a *physical* comparison between man and dog and is unrelated to the dog's *mental* development. If you wait until a dog is one year old before he is trained, then you are going to have some terrible problems. My own experiences indicate that the mental ratio is more like eighteen-to-one: a one-year-old dog can perform on the relative level of an eighteen-yearold boy.

You want a dog that comes to you like a clean slate. This is possible, up to a point. For many reasons, the dog must stay with his mother and his littermates for the first weeks of his life. Not until he's seven weeks old will he be big enough physically to be weaned and safely leave the mother.

Living those first few weeks with his littermates is also very important for other reasons as well. Dogs that have been taken away from the litter before the fourth week often grow not even to know they are dogs. They develop sexual problems and often can never reproduce. During the seven-week period the dog learns a sense of competition in the litter, but the social order—known to the scientists as the pecking order—hasn't as yet had time to form his personality completely. Sensitivity and bullheadedness are not inborn; they're made. It all starts with the interaction in the litter. The runt learns that to get food he may have to fight for it. Another pup gets hurt and shies away. The big one pushes his weight around, and if allowed to continue, he'll become bullheaded. At the other end of the order will be the wallflower. The little personality traits start to develop and may become a hindrance to training. The experience of living in the litter is necessary, but too much of it can be harmful.

At seven weeks of age the pup must start his socializing with humans. This is the time, as we have seen, when the strongest bond can be knit between the dog and his master, and it's also the time when he is most eager to learn. The key to training a dog is to set up the correct environment and get the dog started with you, his master, just as soon as he is physically able to leave the litter. You should be ready to have full control over his development.

What has taken the guesswork out of training a dog has primarily been the work done at the Animal Behavior Laboratory at Hamilton Station, which is part of the Roscoe B. Jackson Memorial Laboratory in Maine. There, while studying the mental development of the dog, the scientists discovered when a dog starts to learn and when training should begin. They learned how important early socialization was to training and what damage the lack of it would do. These discoveries were made in the course of research being done by the laboratory for Guide Dogs for the Blind, Inc. Dogs being taught to guide blind people receive the most rigorous and exacting training of any canines. Guide Dogs for the Blind found itself faced with a serious problem: they couldn't get enough qualified dogs to meet the demand. The way they had always worked in the past was to breed litters of pups for this training from their very best stock. Their experience was, however, that only about 20 percent of these specially bred puppies had the ability to go through the rigorous training program.

Instead of attacking this problem from the breeding standpoint, the scientists at the Roscoe B. Jackson Laboratory investigated a new training method. In one word, it was *acceleration*.

Their investigations showed that there are five critical periods in a pup's life, that his mental development progresses through five distinct phases—all before he reaches the age of sixteen weeks. They found that by this time—much earlier than had been anticipated—the dog's brain has reached its full adult size. The scientists' work proved that waiting for a pup to grow up physically before he was trained was actually harmful.

Beginning the training early gave the experimenters sensational results. Using their accelerated program with the same type of litters from which the breeders had formerly had only 20 percent success in the rigorous training for guide work, the researchers got 90 percent success! In a year's trial at the Seeing-Eye training kennels the success rate was 94 percent.

This early training method can be applied to all breeds of dogs, and the behaviorist can tell you to the exact day what level an animal's mental development has reached.

The scientists break down the development into these five critical periods.

FIRST CRITICAL PERIOD—BIRTH TO 21st DAY

The first twenty-one days of a pup's life is the first critical period. During these three weeks the pup has almost no mental capacity. Only primal needs—for nourishment, sleep, his mother—activate him. Then, suddenly, on the twenty-first day of the pup's life, no matter what his breed, his mentality seems to start functioning. It's as though all the electrical appliances in a house had been waiting for the current to be switched on to start everything operating. This marks the start of the second critical period in the pup's mental development.

SECOND CRITICAL PERIOD—21st TO 28th DAY

From the twenty-first to the twenty-eighth day the pup passes through the second phase. During these seven days he continues to need his mother. His senses function; his brain and nervous system are developing. He is easily frightened by the new impressions that are now coming at him, and he is unusually sensitive to stress of a social or emotional nature. Taking him away from his mother during this week could have a devastating effect.

THIRD CRITICAL PERIOD—28th TO 49th DAY

During this period the pup gradually starts making little trips away from his mother's warmth to explore his surroundings. By the forty-ninth day his brain and nervous system have attained adult capacity, though naturally he's still almost completely inexperienced. He's ready now to begin recognizing humans and responding to their voices. At the same time, he has now lived in the litter long enough to know he is a dog. During these fifth to seventh weeks the pecking order among the pups in the litter has started to be established. The puppy now starts learning, and it is important that at the end of this period you should get into the picture to begin teaching him and molding him as you want him to develop, instead of having his littermates ruin his personality for you.

It is during this third period that the temperament test is run to pick your pup from the litter. By choosing the pup with the best indicated temperament, and by combining with that the starting of the dog's training at this moment when he is most receptive, you will have stacked all the cards in your favor.

FOURTH CRITICAL PERIOD—49th TO 84th DAY

The scientists have found that the best time to begin the dog-human relationship is on the forty-ninth day, not a week earlier or a week later. This is when trainer and pup should get to know one another. The trainer will now, for all practical purposes, assume the place of the puppy's mother. By feeding him, playing with him, and caring for him during these five weeks the trainer will form a lasting bond with the pup. Never again will the dog be able to establish as strong a relationship with any human being. The research at the Animal Behavior Laboratory showed that human contact in this seven-to-twelve-week period was almost the whole key to the dog's future prospects.

During this fourth period, also, we can begin to teach simple commands such as SIT, STAY, COME, and possibly HEEL, though only in the form of games. No discipline should be used on the puppy, but by the eighty-fourth day he'll know what these commands mean.

Extremely important in the pup's mental development at this stage is getting him settled settled in his new home and environment. A puppy who's free from anxieties and feels secure will be receptive to training and discipline.

On the other hand, the animal behaviorists have found that puppies can also develop a condition known as "kennel blindness." They merely exist, in an automatic round of eating and sleeping, waiting for somebody to buy them and give them a home. The experiment has been made by keeping dogs, under laboratory conditions, entirely without human contact during their first sixteen weeks. Such dogs prove to have little chance of ever developing into good companions. Even thirteen weeks without human contact can make puppies untrainable as working dogs.

If lessons and human contacts are started early, but then interrupted for even two or three weeks during which the pup is put back in the kennel, his chances of succeeding in the rigorous training needed to make him a Guide Dog have been found to be drastically lessened. It's important in all training to keep the lessons going.

FIFTH CRITICAL PERIOD—84th TO 112th DAY

From the age of twelve weeks to sixteen weeks the fun and games stop and the young dog starts his serious schooling. Now he is ready to learn disciplined behavior. This is the time, too, when he'll assert his independence and when the question of who's going to be boss—trainer or dog—needs to be settled. If it's deferred till later it may take such drastic methods to settle it that they'd be harmful.

At this time we prepare the puppy for learning. At twelve weeks fundamental training begins, and by the end of sixteen weeks the dog will know his basic commands and respond to them.

What we've tried to do here with this scientific information is to relate it to the training of a house pet. Many people who have such pets may argue that they got their dogs at the age of six months, a year, or whatever, and declare what fine pooches they have. What they say may be true, but they don't know how much better their dogs could have been. By starting your dog at the right age, you'll be taking the luck out of success.

THE DOG'S WAY OF LEARNING

How does a dog learn? The same way a child does. He's got to like the teacher and the school. Even the proverbial old dog, if he's started his education at the right age in puppyhood, retains the capacity to learn all his life.

The animal behaviorists have tested many breeds and have concluded that no one breed is more intelligent than another. It has been shown that a pup that has had plenty of early human contact, and therefore is not people-shy, can use all his intelligence in a learning situation. The same thing applies to what the scientists call "place learning." Place learning goes hand in hand with socialization. If the dog is not frightened in his environment, he will be able to use his natural intelligence in learning and not spend his time dealing with his fears. This is very important in bringing a dog up where there are so many unnatural stresses and strains.

First impressions are very important, and a pup's first experience as soon as he leaves the litter has to be a satisfying one. He will like you from the beginning . . . that's only natural; but you must see that he encounters the new experiences and excitement in such a way that he won't be frightened. By putting him in the surroundings from the very beginning he will learn to accept all the strangeness as being very natural.

One thing comes built into all dogs . . . a strong desire to please. In return they want the master's display of pleasure. This will become an important training tool, and during those early days in the new environment the display of pleasure to comfort the dog can get him over his first rough experiences. For example, on those first few rides in an elevator, a pup that receives a few kind words and a pat will use his native intelligence to realize, "Well, that wasn't so bad." He'll come to accept this as a part of his life and have no fear.

Once we get the socialization and place learning period over with, the dog's desire to please will really be your most valuable asset in training. A dog responds strongly to his master's display of pleasure and displeasure, and since a dog can't speak your language, he learns to read your moods. He can tell your response without a word being spoken. In learning situations there is always tension between the teacher and the student. Reward reduces the tension and gives pleasure. Reprimand or punishment increases the tension and produces discomfort. The dog's instinctive desire to please you leads him to seek your approval. The more strongly you can reinforce the puppy's desire to please, the easier it will be to train him. His urge to please you is heightened by the fact that when his training is started at the age of seven weeks, in the form of games, it is you who love and care for him. At that stage you don't reprimand him for a mistake. So the learning process starts, and later, as it progresses, your common sense should guide you to a proper balance between reward and punishment that will keep the process going. He learns through repetition, with the lessons being repeated over and over until the behavior becomes habitual.

There are two distinct levels on which a dog can learn, the conscious and the unconscious. The latter refers to what the pup learns, without even realizing that he is being taught anything, through repetition of a situation so often that his reaction to it becomes a habit. There is no reprimand or reward; the dog just does what he's expected to do because he has never done it any other way.

For example, he'll learn which is your apartment door without having to be taught it. He'll learn the members of your family the same way. If you take his food away after a respectable length of time, he'll learn that he'll have to eat it when it's put down. If, when you walk him on the street and you stop at the curb before you cross, you give the leash a slight tug to get his attention, he'll learn without a word said that he's to stop before crossing the street. He'll learn that parked cars are not threatening and moving ones make a noise and mean danger. With a little assurance from you he won't mind the roar that comes up from the street subway grating.

The second level of learning, conscious learning, refers to what the dog learns through regular training, discipline, and repetition of lessons until they become a customary part of his behavior. We'll take a closer look at learning on this level in the next chapter.

4. TRAINING PSYCHOLOGY

Being a dog and just wallowing around the house could be really boring if a dog couldn't always get into some mischief. In the mornings he can chew on a curtain or the leg of a chair. If left alone all day, while the master is out at work, he can pass his time walking around the property and tinkling just to warn any other dogs that might come to the house that the joint is his. Of course that leaves plenty of time to sleep in the master's chair and to do the odd jobs such as emptying wastepaper baskets or getting into the garbage.

A trained animal, just like a trained person, is going to be a much happier individual. Good citizenship is the first order of business, and that doesn't come built into any animal. Furnishing protection, which is becoming more and more of a concern to the master, can be an extremely important job and one any dog can learn, using our system. We might not think of companionship as a job, but in our society that too is very important. Needing a friend at one's beck and call in the cold cliffs of a city is a real part of the emotional make-up of man. Age doesn't seem to be a factor. For some senior citizens, the dog provides the only outlet for their expression of love. Also, everyone wants to feel needed. For a child, training a dog is a good educational experience. Whatever your reason for having or wanting a dog, it's important to give your pup a job; he'll be happier if he, too, feels needed.

THE TEACHING ROLE

A smart dog will try to take advantage of his teacher. Most dogs go untrained because the trainer is not consistent, and like a child, the dog will try to get away with murder. If he can succeed in getting his way once, he will keep testing to see if he can do it again. He'll be learning, all right, but it will be the wrong thing.

He's keen at feeling out a training situation and putting on a sad look, a put-on pose, hoping that you'll melt and stop the lesson. So many people quit, saying that their dog is too sensitive. People forget that learning is never easy and the only way to be successful as a trainer is to keep the pupil-teacher relationship rigid while school is in session.

A good way to start any training, whether a formal lesson or a corrective measure around the house, is to call the dog firmly by name. A short name is always best. The firm voice will convey to the pup that you mean business, and using his name will get you his attention. Always win your point while training; you must retain the authority at all times. Your voice will have much to do with your success and failure. Firmness sprinkled with affection will soon teach the dog that he can't evade the lesson, and with plenty of praise when he does well, he'll learn to enjoy learning.

Confidence is the key to training. We start with the pup at a very early age so that we can earn his confidence. The first thing we do is to take the place of the mother in the pup's world. We feed him, give him water, keep him warm, and give him a snug bed. Of course, he is going to like us, and showing his pleasure is a built-in response. As his "mother," you now have the opportunity to mold the desired personality in the dog.

Training is really very simple. First you have to know what you want the dog to do; then you have to make sure he understands what is expected of him. Here is where you have to be consistent. Always teach whatever command it is in the same way. Don't be changeable. Use the same voice commands, the same body motions, each time.

A dog is very practical and has no moral sense. He'll use any method he can to achieve what he wants. If he knows the rule around the dining room is no food from the table and gives you the sad-eye treatment, and you renege just once by feeding him a tidbit, you have lost an important step in the training. He gets more than the food in that case; he learns that you can be begged into a change of mind. If it happens once, there is no reason for him to assume that it won't happen again. Actually, you have broken the confidence line in the training by that one slip.

SOME WORDS ABOUT REPRIMAND

Make sure throughout the training that the dog knows what is expected of him before you reprimand him. There is no faster way to destroy his confidence in you than by punishing him for something he didn't realize was wrong. Remember, a young dog has practically no memory, so you'll have to be Johnny-on-the-spot with the reprimand.

In the temperament tests we found that some dogs were of a dominant nature and some had a tendency to be timid. By taking a timid dog from the litter early, he can be brought around to some degree. But the dog's natural temperament should be kept in mind when he is being trained. The dominant dog will need a firm hand. The pup that came up with a good many #3's in his score will need a lighter hand, and the shy one will have to be handled with care. It is important to recognize when you have "reached" the dog during a reprimand. You can tell by his tail drooping or his ears lying down. A defiant personality makes a dog tough to train. The point is that no matter what his temperament, the dog will have to be reprimanded at some point in his early training. Punishment should fit his temperament and the crime; this is the part of training on which most people fail.

Remember that a pup that has just been brought home should go through his training for the next four weeks without any reprimand . . . his learning is in the form of play-type games. From the twelfth to the sixteenth week, school is in formal session, and reprimand takes the form of firm handling. It's not until this period is over, when the dog knows all his commands, that any physical reprimand should be given. At this point, if you have followed this book and the time schedule for the training, he'll know what is expected and what the commands mean.

Almost every writer will have a different approach. Some tell you never, but never, to hit a dog. One book says never to lay a hand on a dog unless he's going to bite someone. It's too late then, as far as I'm concerned. A dog should never be allowed to get that far before he feels the sting of a spanking. (Which reminds me of the beggar who approached a man walking his dog and said, "Excuse me, sir, I haven't had a bite in weeks." You know what happened.)

Some object to spanking a dog, thinking he'll become hand-shy. This won't happen if you handle it correctly. A dog doesn't resent a spanking if he knows he's done wrong. He'll learn that the hand that cares for him, feeds him, and pats him when he's obedient is the same hand that stings him when he becomes obstreperous.

Some suggest the rolled newspaper. In my opinion this is very cruel. It's wrong to teach a dog to fear a loud noise. A dog can be conditioned this way, become noise-shy and end up a nervous wreck. Reprimand has to be given immediately, not after the act when you've found wherever you've left your rolled-up newspaper. Also, is it any wonder why paperboys and postmen delivering papers get the seats of their pants taken out?

There's a vast difference between a dog lover and a dog trainer. A trainer can combine two things . . . loving his dog and having a well-behaved and well-trained companion. People seem to forget that love alone will produce a spoiled dog . . . discipline is necessary, too.

Everyone knows how to express love to a dog; a pat, a caress, a few kind words . . . dogs eat it up. But the reprimand is quite tricky. From the moment the dog enters his new home with you he's going to hear one command, and he'll continue to hear it the rest of his life: it's the command NO. The whole purpose of training is to diminish the use of this command. By the time the puppy is an adult he'll know what's expected of him, and the command will very seldom be necessary.

There are many forms and degrees of reprimand. Often, you can punish a dog just as effectively by ignoring him as by spanking him. For example, if you're teaching him the command STAY and instead he comes, he'll expect you to make a fuss over him and praise him. Instead, give him the silent treatment. Take him back to his original position and start him over again. Ignoring him hurts his self-esteem.

If you suspect that a dog understands what you want him to do but is just being lazy or stubborn, it sometimes helps to come at him with an upraised hand. A hat is sometimes effective as the threatening weapon. However, this approach calls for careful judgment. You should consider the circumstances, the dog's age, and other pertinent factors, and decide whether he should have known better . . . then mete out the punishment if warranted.

If the dog gets downright uncooperative and stubborn, there's only one way to straighten him out. Thrash him, but do it intelligently. Use a folded leash until he cries out once. Talk angrily until after the outcry. Then return to a pleasant tone of voice and go on with the lesson. Get things back to normal as quickly as possible. Sentimentalists may think this clear-cut discipline harsh, but it isn't. It's kinder than not disciplining a dog.

HIS MASTER'S VOICE

Dogs never understand our language as we know it: they work mainly from the tone of the words. They're geniuses at interpreting sounds. Their sensitive ears are irritated by harsh tones. Low, conversational tones encourage a puppy. However, you shouldn't beg him to obey or—heaven forbid—use baby talk to a pup. You're giving a command, not making a request, so speak with authority.

The commands should be short, clear-cut words like SIT, STAY, COME, NO. Don't make your commands confusing by adding a lot of verbiage to them. Don't say, "SIT, fellow . . . come along . . . no, no, let's try it once more. Here now, Tar, SIT." In that example we just wanted to have the dog SIT, but in the confusing jabber no fewer than four commands were given: SIT, NO, COME, Tar. His name is really a command to give you his attention.

Dog training is largely a matter of communication. There are only about ten words that your dog is going to learn, but he'll learn hundreds of intonations. The tone of your voice can tell the dog your meaning, so you've got to know what tone to use. Consistency in communicating is the key to all animal training. You must be consistent in maintaining a balance between praise and correction. It's up to you to feel your way along to determine when each should be used. A command-giving voice should be firm, sharp, authoritative. A praising voice should have an easy lilt, a softness. A flat tone of praise won't bring the joyous response from the dog that he wants to give.

Sometimes a dog will test your patience by stalling before he responds to a command. Show him he can't get away with this. A good rousing "Hey you! What's going on?" will jerk him out of it.

ANIMAL SENSE

We can do all the talking we want about the dog's learning habits, his mental development, and all the other things that you have read so far, but how do we tell you about developing your animal sense? It means more than just under-standing and recognizing the problems that the dog has. A good teacher will put himself in the place of the student and then know how to proceed. No book can anticipate all the situations that will pop up and give you answers on how to deal with them. Although we will try, a lot will still depend on you. As the teacher, you will have to make fast decisions when certain situations arise. You will have to develop a feel for just how far to go. The age of the dog must be considered. The circumstances have to be taken into account. It's a good rule to say that you should never let a dog get away with any variation in performance. For example, if a pup finds an old slipper and chews on it, and you don't correct him, what do you think will happen when he finds your best new shoes? When you get angry at him he's going to be some confused pup. To be a dog trainer you are going to have to be able to put yourself in both places. Since he can't talk to you, you'll have to see things from the dog's side too.

When it comes to the formal training in the commands, stick to the simple lessons and repeat them over and over until his response is automatic, then build on each command. For example, don't try to teach DOWN before the pup learns the command SIT. (We'll take up these and other "moving commands" in detail in the next chapter.) Don't push a pup too far to show what a good trainer you are or how smart your pup is. I have seen trainers push three-month-old pups and get themselves into a bind because they wouldn't give an inch. There is a point when a trainer ought to have more sense and see that the dog has had enough for the time being. The smart trainer will stop before he reaches the bind. How does the trainer know? That's animal sense, and the only thing an author can tell you is that you have to think ahead and use common sense.

How do you know when you have gone too far with the lessons? When school is in session, some trainers suggest training by the clock and arbitrarily say lessons should last ten minutes. I do it by the tail instead of the clock. The tail is a very good indicator of a dog's attitude. A high tail means he's still with you, and a low tail means he's had it for the day. You have to get to know your dog, since some will be more receptive to school than others. Chances are, if your dog doesn't like his lessons it means that you went too far one day and took the spirit for the classroom out of him. On the other hand, when he puts on a hurt look, by quitting the lessons you might have shown him how to get out of class. You took that look for his having had enough. That's known as a sensitive dog . . . sensitive, my eye. That's a smart dog who is getting around you. There is a definite expression around the eyes of a confused dog—a worried look. That should tell you that the dog is not sure of you or what you want. That's your signal to ease up and start back over things he knows.

Don't nag the dog to death. If you do, he'll respond just as a child will . . . he'll tune you out. Learning is fun for a while, but too much makes it a bloody bore. If he's bored, let up on the training for a day or so and have him do only the things he already knows and likes to do. All pups, like kids, go through a teenage period. If you think he's only expressing his independence, be cautious but firm. Win each battle, but not harshly . . . you only want to teach him who is boss, in as kindly a way as possible. Although it's possible to train too much, it's never possible to play too much.

A pup will tune you out when he discovers you don't know what you are doing. The pictures of the girl in the park are so typical. Her pup ran to play with another young one who was on leash. She should never have let her dog run free because she had absolutely no control over him. The pup just tuned her out and stayed out of her reach. It was all a big game to him. She finally gained control when she cornered him and lunged at him. She never did follow through with all the terrible things she said she was going to do when she caught him. This isn't just lack of animal sense . . . it's stupid dog handling. If people handle their

So many people show a lack of understanding in dealing with an animal. Her pup was bothering the man, who had his dog under control. She tried to grab her dog and when she did grab him, she never corrected him or followed through with all she said she was going to do. Children who are handled this way end up as spoiled brats . . . dogs are no different.

dogs—or babies—like that, both kinds of youngsters have a difficult time when they come up against a structured society where they have to conform.

I introduce this kind of teaching behavior because if you, the reader, handle training problems on this emotional level and expect to get results, you will fail. The way to learn to teach is to force yourself into a structured plan, which will be set up for you in these pages.

COMMUNICATIONS

Some men can stand on the street, look you right in the eye, and tell you the biggest lie in the world; you would have to know them pretty well to know they weren't telling the truth. No dog has that ability. We humans have come to depend on verbal communication for so long that we've all but lost the use of our other sensory organs. A dog is still in the primitive state as far as that is concerned. He learns to observe better than we do and uses all his senses when dealing with us. A gesture, an attitude, a smell, a sound, all become part of his decision-making apparatus. He'll size up a total situation and then respond. His response will be honest. There is no way for him to say one thing and mean another. We might be able to fool other men with our language, but you can't fool a dog. Even a child is often harder to fool than a grown man. When you say to a small child, "I'll spank you if you do it again," the child reads more than just the words. He, like a dog, can tell if you really mean it. There are times when he is not sure and will test the situation. Then you have to put up or shut up. As a dog's teacher, if you remember this you'll get better results. Your pup will always deal honestly with you. He may not want to do what you want, but he'll let you know that too. Remember that dealing with a dog is like dealing with an infant . . . communication is very direct.

THE SCHOOL FOR TEACHERS

I've been trying to show you why it's best for the pup that his training be started at the forty-ninth day and carried through his last two critical mental development periods under your guidance. There is another important reason and it concerns you. We've just talked about animal sense. Many people don't have it naturally, but those who don't can acquire it by using this early training method. Actually, as you will see, we will be training according to the age of the pup. There will be three distinct phases to the training. They are: the five weeks of training when it's like kindergarten—all fun and games; the next four weeks when formal school starts and corrections begin; and the last phase when the dog goes on and had better obey and get his advanced training.

It's during the early phases of the training that the new trainer gets his animal sense. He will learn much about the personality of the pup. During this period the learning has to be a two-way street. Since you must not reprimand the pup except with the command NO during the first five weeks, you will learn how well you do as a teacher. By the time he is twelve weeks old he will sit, stay, and come on command. If he is not doing it, your animal sense needs some overhauling. I won't be able to assist you much with that . . . you will have to think it out yourself to see what you are doing wrong. Don't assume that the dog is not doing well. Are *you* consistent? Are you trying to take him too fast? Does the dog understand what you want? Do you get emotional? Do you lose your temper? Are you too passive? But even more important at this time are questions like: Does the dog respond to a stern voice? Does he like to play games? When you make him do a lesson over is his tail up? Does he show spunk after he's made to sit and stay? You must learn to read the signs the dog gives so that when the lessons progress to the next phase you'll understand how much both of you can take without getting upset. You are asking the dog to learn step by step, and this is your opportunity to do the same thing.

The advantage here is simple . . . step-by-step learning from the beginning gives you the time to observe and see how well you are doing. You are not going to make a major blunder if you follow the simple plan. I'll show you what to expect and how to proceed. Starting a pup from scratch means that he comes with no problems built in. You have the chance to mold the kind of pupil you want.

WHO IS THE TRAINER IN THE FAMILY?

Every member of the family should learn how to handle the dog, but it's best during the early phases of training to have one person do the training. Once the dog learns the commands, then the trainer should show each member of the family how to do it. Everything should be done as consistently as possible to avoid confusion on the dog's part. Don't rush to have the other members of the family become teachers; there will be plenty of time for that. Don't have them around when "class" is in session. There will be too many distractions, and cross conversations will ruin the pup's attentiveness.

Explain as much as you can about how the pup is being trained so that other members of the family don't think you are being unkind and don't get into the act secretly and upset all that is being done. We have a chance here to shape a personality and a behavior that we want. Someone who is interfering like a doting "grandmother" could spoil a lot of work. It's so hard to mold our children because we have so much interference from other members of society who get involved. Teachers, aunts, uncles, even husbands and wives, have different opinions. How many times have you observed a child get a spanking and then seen the child run to another member of the family for sympathy . . . which he receives? That child doesn't learn the lesson of the spanking . . . he learns to get his way. No matter how smart that child is, if he's spoiled he could learn to hate school when he comes up against a firm teacher who won't let him run away for sympathy. Dogs are no different.

The man who trains a hunting or working dog does all the training himself because he knows that commands are conveyed to the dog by more than words and hand signals. For example, a dog reads all the body motions associated with training. The pup can tell by a stance, a gesture, a facial expression, a tone, whether or not you mean business. Each person will show such signs in a different way, so it is best for the dog that one person do the basic training.

THINK LIKE A DOG

Thinking like a dog isn't easy for some people I know. Often problems arise in training, and we apply human values to them, only to discover that a dog has different standards. One person I know had a Great Dane who was acquired as a grown dog and couldn't get the idea that he was to do his business outside. After a number of mistakes the trainer, upset by all the mess in the house, decided to take stronger action. On the next occasion the dog was hustled off to an empty room and tied up very short by his leash. After an appropriate period of time he was released. Later that day the dog made another mistake, but instead of feeling ashamed, off he ran to the empty room and stood in his corner wagging his tail to be tied up. Obviously that dog didn't consider being tied up so bad . . . he liked it.

Another dog owner had a problem with his poodle. Every time he got a chance the dog would run away and be gone for hours. He seemed to enjoy himself on his jaunts. The master took what he thought was a corrective measure; he confined the dog. This only made the poodle want to get out more than ever, and he did. In this case the punishment only made things worse. If that trainer had been thinking like a dog, he'd have realized that the animal needed more exercise instead of less.

A trainer can't ask a dog questions and get answers, so he's got to figure out what motivates the animal. For example, does a pup that chews do it because he is bored, or is he teething? If the trainer can figure out the dog's motivation, he usually solves the problems . . . and thinking like a dog helps.

Can you imagine what this dog could do to a house if he were not a good citizen?

5. FIRST STAGES IN TRAINING
THE HOME DOG

HOW TO START . . . USE A ONE-ROOM SCHOOLHOUSE

Once we've brought the pup home to the big new kennel, how do we start his training? Don't give him the run of the whole house. When he lived with his brothers and sisters he lived in a confined area, and he should be started off the same way in your house. How long he stays in these quarters really depends on how fast he learns a few simple facts about life in the new place. Being very democratic, a pup will soil an Oriental rug just as soon as making a biological comment about the editorial page of *The New York Times*. As soon as he decides that the *Times* is better than the rug, he may be allowed to have the run of the house.

The kitchen is the best room in the house for the one-room school since it's the place where the most activity goes on. A screen across the doorway makes it

The best smells are in the kitchen and there is usually someone around. It's the easiest room to keep clean; it makes a good one-room house.

a fine playpen. It has the nicest smells of all the rooms and is the easiest to keep clean. At the pup's level, there isn't much he can do to cause damage or get hurt.

One corner of the room can be made into his bedroom. It should be free of drafts and have a soft mat. The bed can be an old rug, a few towels, or a cloth bag filled with cedar chips. It really won't make much difference; he'll like whatever you can give him, and he'll do a lot of sleeping the first month or so.

Getting acclimated is an important part of the puppy's training. What is he learning? Right from the start he'll learn to like you. You'll develop in him a sense of security. At the same time you'll impose on him mild restrictions and irritations that will develop his tolerance. Giving the pup a sense of security and providing him with an opportunity to develop a tolerance to the world is the way to build the foundations of a well-balanced dog.

Human contact at the age of seven to twelve weeks is as important to the training at this time as formal lessons are later. Remember, the behaviorists have proved that without this early human contact dogs lose the ability to be trained. This is such an easy part of the process. Who can resist a fluffy pup? Feed him, keep him warm, play with him, love him, and see that he doesn't get hurt. In return he'll love you, and that starts to create the right kind of bond between you.

Many professional dog people have taken issue with this early training. The reason is obvious. The behaviorists say that the dog must have his human contact started at the forty-ninth day. The dog seller tries to brush this information aside as unimportant. It would mean that he would have to have sales for the litter in advance, and it rarely works out that way. The fact is that a dog that sits around in the kennel until he is three months old has missed the chance to have the most important part of his mental development with you. Actually, there is a way around all this, as the Guide Dog trainers have found. People who run kennels or pet shops could give these pups their socialization each day. All they would have to do is play with the pups or hire school kids to come in twice a day and play with the pups individually. Introducing the pups to a homelike situation for a few minutes each day would certainly give both the pups and the purchasers a head start. This takes an extra effort and some work on the part of the breeder. It seems so much simpler to leave a pup and his kennel mates together until someone comes along to buy the pup. But the longer that situation lasts after the seventh week, the more damage is being done, . . . and the future success of the training is jeopardized as each day goes by.

Socialization is so easy; the time it takes would pay off to the dog sellers. The chance of the new owner's success is increased dramatically by giving the little human attention a dog needs during this critical period. It was found in experiments run at the Animal Behavior Laboratory that five minutes twice a day made all the difference in the world. The added investment of money and time involved keeps many of the breeders from doing anything about this problem.

Breeders like to stress conformation and heredity. But training and environment are far more important for a well-trained dog. How those early weeks are handled can be the determining factor affecting a dog's whole life.

Professional dog breeders and trainers are often heard to say, "Oh, a fine pup, very well bred, but a little sensitive." Sensitive, my eye. The pup is insecure, and he wasn't born that way. Your first job—the first part of the training—is to make your pup a happy one. A happy pup will take to his lessons easily . . . so get into the act early or make sure someone else does.

PUTTING UP WITH IRRITATIONS

For any child or pup there is a balance between getting one's own way and accepting a certain amount of discomfort that will prepare him for a healthy life. Those children who always get what they want grow to be spoiled brats, while if they get only abuse they will become antisocial delinquents. It's no different with pups. Security and care are very important, but sprinkled in with them should be a certain amount of discomfort. Life is not a bed of roses, and the pup that learns this while being cared for will be ready to accept your training when the time comes.

After the pup has been in the new home for a few days, and as soon as you are sure that all is going well, put a collar on him for a short time each day. It'll be an irritant, but he'll survive. Later you can add a leash and let him drag it around the house.

There will be times in the one-room schoolhouse when the pup will be under foot and in the way. By tying his leash to the doorknob, you can easily take care

Not getting his own way is part of the training. He finally accepted the situation.

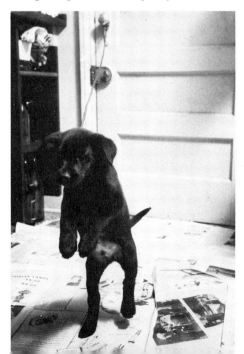

of that problem. The pup is not going to like it, but he'll soon learn to handle the situation . . . by sleeping. This is the kind of irritant that we suggest. It doesn't hurt the dog physically, but he is learning an important part of life. If he learns to accept mild irritations now, it follows that he'll take to his training easier later.

GO TO BED . . . A KIND OF RESTRICTION

The one-room schoolhouse is also the bedroom for the pup. Having the pup sleep with you is a mistake. It usually gets started because the first night that the pup is with you, nobody sleeps. He doesn't like the loneliness and lets the whole family hear about his plight. Sometime in the wee hours the pup, with his bed and all, are brought to the bedroom, and you try to get some sleep with your hand in the box. All you are really doing is putting the problem off to a future night. The makeshift first night arrangement teaches the pup that if he barks and carries on he'll get his way and end up in the bedroom where all the folks seem to be.

Some people suggest giving the dog an alarm clock or a hot water bottle to sleep with. For us that procedure has only led to either a broken clock or a leaky water bag. There is no way to avoid his being lonely. You might as well get ready —both of you—for a few nights of bad sleep.

Start the pup in his bed in the kitchen and make it a rule not to go to him— that's what he wants you to do—no matter how sad he sounds. Let him howl it out. If he doesn't bark himself to sleep command QUIET through the door. Don't go into his room to give the command. It may not work, but it'll calm your 3:30 A.M. nerves and let the dog know that he really is not alone. If he continues to carry on, rap on the door and in a firm voice tell him, "Quiet in there!" Stand by the door. When he thinks you are gone and starts up again, just rap on the door.

The first few nights are the worst. After that he may try a few ineffectual howls as a protest. He's just hoping you'll change your mind and come and sleep with him. Don't renege . . . have a little more patience. It's not only the pupil who has to put up with a few irritations. Take a sleeping pill, and more important, try to be human at breakfast.

Irritations should not include any kind of abuse. Children, if not watched, can be cruel and play too hard with a pup. They have to be taught what they can and can't do. They must be given a certain amount of responsibility for their behavior and also the pup's.

HOUSEBREAKING

Housebreaking means different things to different people. To a thief it means getting into the house, to a dog owner it means getting out of it. To the young pup it means a certain amount of confusion, but that is solved by the one-room schoolhouse.

Many dog trainers suggest that paper training for a pup is not a good technique, but in the city paper training, started at the age of seven weeks, is a must. You can't take a young pup out on the street where he will come into contact with other dogs until your vet tells you the pup's shots will protect him from distemper. The one-room schoolhouse becomes a place where the pup will automatically train himself to the paper method.

In very short order the puppy will learn where he is to sleep, and by instinct he will decide that his bathroom should be at the other end of the room. When the pup is first brought home, the whole kitchen floor is covered with many thick layers of newspaper. The papers should be picked up as soon as he has soiled them. Not all the papers should be removed. Take up the ones that are soiled, but leave the lower sheets that still retain some of the odor. You will not smell it, but the pup will. That will encourage him to go back to the same area the next time. If he starts to use a place that is not convenient for you, move those bottom papers to the area of your choice. He'll get the point.

Once the "place" is established, you can start to reduce the area that is covered with paper, and before you know it you'll be down to a corner of the room. When you see the pup going toward the area with sniffing on his mind, a few soft words of encouragement will speed his learning.

Once the vet gives you permission to take the dog out for his walk, a few sheets of paper will soon teach him what the walk is for. This housebreaking routine is not as difficult as it might seem. Actually, puppies do very well on this score. It takes a human puppy two years to become housebroken; a dog will learn what is expected in a few weeks and be able to control himself completely by the time he is four months old. Those people who buy an older dog or one that they can walk immediately could have more serious problems than housebreaking . . . older dogs usually come with someone else's problems built in.

Learning what the paper is for will take only a week, and we've had some dogs that learned it in a matter of days. For working people who leave a dog all day in an apartment this method becomes an emergency standby, even when the dog is an adult. Many people like to keep their dogs paper-trained so that they can travel with a pet more easily.

Of course, a dog is going to make mistakes. You have to be Johnny-on-the-spot. If you see he is about to make or has begun the accident, shout "No!" and pick him up and rush him to the paper. This is rather traumatic, so be sure to praise him when he has accomplished what you want. Don't rub his nose in his mistake, as some trainers suggest. It won't accomplish a thing, and it's rather disgusting.

Keep a small area covered with paper even if you are not going to continue this method. He may get the idea fast that the outside makes a better bathroom, but a young pup does not have complete control over his bowels. Paper should be left down at night and for accidents during the day.

Transferring the act to the outside can be easy, but if there is a problem it's because you haven't communicated properly with the dog to show him what the walks are for. Your vet will give you feeding instructions for your dog. Make it a routine to feed him on schedule, then take him for his walk. You will have to watch the dog after he eats to learn about how long it takes before he starts to give the signal that he is going to have a bowel movement. The reason for finding out his schedule is to make the walks as short as possible. Get the pup outside just before he has to go, and then praise him for his act. Immediately after the praise take him back to the house. That way he'll learn what the walks are for. Eating, drinking, and walks should be on a very tight schedule.

Walk the pup on a long leash for this purpose . . . some dogs are shy. Don't jerk the leash to encourage him. Be patient and talk to him softly. Take him back to the same place where he went before. Once he does his business show him you are pleased.

If you have a very specific problem that will cause embarrassment for you—for instance, if you are visiting someone—a glycerine suppository will get things started no matter what the schedule is.

For those who want to keep the paper method as a way of life for the dog, the newspaper can be transferred to the outside by taking a few sheets from the

When you are sure he knows better but he decides to take the easy way out and use the rug . . . give him what for! You have to catch him in the act; then he'll learn to give you a signal to go out.

kitchen that still have an odor on them outside to the yard. Let the dog sniff the paper, and if you make these paper-carrying trips on schedule, he'll learn soon what it's all about.

For those dogs that have a hard time learning the transfer from kitchen to the outside, the paper method can assist in teaching the dog what you expect him to do. A few sheets at the curb will quickly show him what you want. Once he gets the idea, eliminate the papers.

A few tips. Don't vary the dog's diet. Don't feed him snacks in-between meals. Take the dog out about five times a day. Be sure walks early in the morning and late at night are on your schedule. Give the pup his meals on a regular timetable, allowing him about fifteen minutes to eat. If he decides to be fussy and not to eat, take up the food. He has to learn the schedule for intake so you can schedule the other end. Follow the vet's feeding and drinking instructions, but to cut down on water intake you can substitute a few ice cubes in his dish during parts of the day. If the dog makes a mistake and you don't catch him in the act, there is no point to punishing him later . . . he just won't be able to put two and two together.

It is important to get rid of any odors of accidents the dog has had around the house. There are special liquid odor neutralizers to do this job. Ordinary household cleaners will not do it. Pet shops carry a number of brands that work.

Some dogs respond to a new place, a different situation, or a break in their routine by becoming nervous or frightened, and they will have an accident. This won't happen if those first few weeks are controlled in the special environment that you have set up.

In this discussion about housebreaking we have been talking about you and your dog. There is a bigger problem in our cities, and it has to do with your neighbors.

THE STREETS . . . WHOSE RESPONSIBILITY?

You wouldn't be reading this book unless you had an affinity for dogs, but dog owners are in the minority in our urban society. A CBS editorial complained about the 300,000 dogs in New York City alone. That's a heck of a lot of dogs to make messes. It's been said that if you lined up all the dogs in New York, elephant fashion, they'd string all the way to Boston . . . and that would even be a lot of elephants.

The Environmental Protection Agency has full-time personnel trying to educate neighborhood organizations on the control of dog litter. They have printed and distributed publications such as the "Dog Owner's Guide to Scooping" and a do-it-yourself self-starter kit in the form of an instructional newspaper that you read and then let your dog use. The problem is getting serious, and lobbies for and against dogs in our urban areas are becoming very active. Actually the problem is not with the dog . . . it's with the people.

Curbing your dog is not too difficult a task, but many dog owners won't even take the trouble to do it. It really is abiding by the Golden Rule, and that is something city dwellers seem to have forgotten. No wonder that newspaper headlines read, "Housing Authority Exiles Dogs From Buildings," and that politicians are getting into the act on both sides of the issue.

The purpose of this book is to teach you to train your dog, and part of that job is to remind you that you do have a responsibility to your own neighborhood. Our environment is what we make it. If the rule is to curb your dog, you should be fined if you do not obey the rule. If it becomes a requirement to clean up after your dog, it should be done. There are devices that can be bought at pet shops that do the job without much fuss.

On the other hand, the dog owner is not the only one who should take some responsibility. We do not make our citizens in general take complete responsibility for other urban problems. The streets in most of our cities rank with the dirtiest in the world. We could have designated dog-walking areas in our cities, just as we provide facilities for other citizens with special interests. New York's Central Park, one of the largest city parks in the world, has one fenced-in dog area, and it's the only one in the city. It does not cover an area of more than a quarter of an acre. Dog groups have gone to the municipal government and asked permission to put up fenced-in walk areas that they would pay for and maintain themselves, but they've been refused. The single area that exists can only serve the people in that one locality near the park.

Housing administrators, too, are quick to keep dogs out, yet they have never approached the problem from a realistic point of view. Provision should be made in the original architectural designs for apartment buildings for dog runs, walking facilities on the roof, and sanitation maintenance.

Dog people can expect that the issue of the dog mess will become a local political football; it should not be treated lightly. If it ever comes to a vote, dogs could be banned from our cities. The way to prevent all this is for each dog owner to take full responsibility and to make sure his dog is not fouling our sidewalks. We've got to think of the other fellow.

The dog can't read signs. It is our responsibility to think of others and keep our sidewalks clean. This problem is getting out of hand and citizens' groups can make it very difficult for our dogs. This little girl did the right thing with her dog . . . we all have to.

6. TEACHING THE BASIC COMMANDS

Learning obedience to six basic commands is a fundamental part of your dog's education. These commands include SIT, STAY, COME, DOWN, and DOWN-STAY, which we shall teach to him in that order. The command NO is of course often needed also. Since the commands often involve walking, and because walking smoothly and quietly with his master is an important accomplishment for a dog, we'll also learn how to train him to make the outside and inside turns. Executing these turns smoothly is a hallmark of the well-trained dog with whom it's a pleasure to stroll down the avenue.

STARTING TO TEACH THE COMMANDS . . .

When does the actual training in the commands start? The first phase of the puppy's training, as we have noted, is just a matter of his getting used to the new place and people. During this time you will be able to determine the exact day to start training your dog in the first command . . . SIT.

Here is the way it'll happen. Each evening after the chores of the day are over, bring the pup into the room with the family for a short time. Not only will this make him feel that he's a member of the family, but you'll be able to observe him. Some of the time can be spent playing with the pup, and then give him time to explore and do his own playing. It's during the period when the whole family is settled down that you test the pup. Repeat this test each evening until you get a response.

Here is the test: while the pup is quietly doing his thing, such as chewing on a toy or a bone, sharply call his name. The first few times there will be no response. Don't call him by name more than once . . . only once. The next evening try the same thing again. To set the test up properly, wait until the pup is facing away from you and diligently working on whatever he has in his mouth before you call him. You are waiting for him to recognize his name and to stop whatever he's doing and turn his head toward you, as much as to say, "What do you want?"

When this happens, at that moment, he's ready to accept his first training . . . and the results will be spectacular. I have found that this happens with pups between the ages of fifty-eight and sixty-five days. That's the time to start the first play lesson, command SIT. Put the leash on him and start to go through the command SIT, which I will explain later. In five minutes he'll get the idea of what you want him to do. Do it only a few times. Try it again an hour or so later. You'll be so pleased at what happened so fast.

STARTING TO TEACH
THE COMMANDS

This is a startling demonstration of how fast a pup will start learning. Top left: he is doing his thing, playing with a glove. Call him by name and when he stops and pays attention (upper right), he's ready. Start the SIT lesson. Within minutes he'll learn SIT and (next page) STAY. It all comes so fast that you will be surprised and when you try it again, you'll see that he remembers. He'll need help, and if you make it fun he'll want to remember.

I remember telling members of a field trial club that I belonged to about this test. They had a lot of fun teasing me about my early recognition system, until one night the meeting was at my home. A new pup was in the house and in the middle of the meeting, while he was across the room, I called the pup by name, and he responded by stopping what he was doing and looking quizzically at me. That ended the meeting. I asked the group if they'd like to see what could be done with the pup who'd just responded to his name. I proceeded to teach the dog SIT, STAY, COME on command. The club members couldn't believe what they were seeing. There was no need to ask any questions . . . they saw it all from the very start. The next night a few of them came back to see what the pup remembered. They were equally impressed the next night because by that time the pup had learned to sit on whistle command.

There is no scientific proof of why pups will start responding favorably to command training sometime between the ages of fifty-eight and sixty-five days, but it's simple and it works . . . the effect is like showing your friends magic tricks.

The work ahead for both you and your dog is going to be a team job. We have discussed a lot of theory and tried to set the stage with practical information for the two of you. Now let's explore in detail a system for training a dog that really works.

First we'll see how a professional handles his dog through the simple commands, and then we'll show you what you can expect. This is what you and your dog will be working toward. Let's start with one of the most important tools used by professional trainers . . . the choke collar.

There is a right and wrong way to use the choke collar. Drop the chain through . . .

THE MISNOMER . . . THE CHOKE COLLAR

The choke collar, which you, too, should use, is the most effective correcting device there is for training dogs. It beats hollering and screaming, chasing, swatting with rolled up newspapers, and even the strap to the hindquarters. The unfortunate thing about it is its name. It can be for choking, but it's not supposed to be used that way. When properly handled it will tighten around the dog's neck and then release quickly without causing any pain. This is called the corrective jerk.

Choke collars come in all sizes. The kind called jeweled choke collars are best because their links, which are so closely assembled that they resemble jewelry, release quickly and smoothly, unlike the wide-linked collars, which can jam. It is not a good idea to leave these collars on all the time, especially with small dogs or pups. Hunting dogs never wear them while they are working because they can catch onto limbs or brush, trap a dog, and possibly strangle him. They're a training tool and should be used when you want the dog under your control. Even with a young pup the choke collar comes to mean "school is in session."

There is a right and wrong way to put the collar on. Let's look at the right way.

. . . the ring and make a loop. Then switch hands, as in upper right picture . . .

. . . slip the loop over his head. Now the chain will tighten or release instantly.

THE CORRECTIVE JERK

One good jerk is better than a lot of nagging little ones. Make the correction and get it over with. Use the command NO with the jerk. It's going to startle the dog more than hurt him. Trainers differ on the force of the jerk. Some say never do it hard enough to lift the dog's feet off the ground. Nonsense. That's like saying, spank a child but not hard enough to make it sting. There are occasions when it's necessary. Here is where your dog sense has to come into play. Obviously, you are not going to be rough on a dog when he is first being taught a command. You can't use the same force on a small dog that you would on a big one. The "front-feet-off-the-ground" jerk is not an everyday occurrence. It is used when you know the dog knows what is wanted, but he has decided for himself to ignore you and the command you are giving. You will see that once the dog has experienced the rough jerk, the choke collar only has to be jiggled, and he'll be Johnny-on-the-spot.

It will become obvious to you when you are training a dog how much force that particular dog needs. The strong-headed ones need a firmer hand than the more sensitive animals. But don't be fooled by the dog that makes a big scene out of a little jerk. That whining or crying out is only a ploy to keep you from jerking the collar; he gets around you and controls the situation.

The corrective jerk is usually done from the right hand. While walking, the leash is slack. The jerk is made by swinging the arm out to the right, then immediately releasing it . . . like a spring. As the pictures show, sometimes two hands are used. Immediately after the correction and his proper response to the command, praise the dog. Next time he'll do what you want to get the praise and not the jerk.

On the opposite page is the problem, the command was HEEL but the dog seems to have other ideas. Above, he's still not responding. So, comes the corrective jerk. With a full grown dog, it's a firm jerk. Show him you mean business; up come his front feet. Below things get back to normal. Then you can show him that he's a good fellow . . . praise him.

TEACHING THE TURNS AND BASIC COMMANDS

In the accompanying photos a professional trainer demonstrates, using a trained dog, how to teach the turns and the basic commands. You'll see in these pictures how the trainer handles each situation. Later photos will show a young pup following the same commands.

The first of these pictures show the outside and inside turns, which are so important for a well-behaved dog. It's no fun to walk with a puller or a lagger. A dog shouldn't be tending to everybody else's business while walking on the street or greeting every passer-by. He has to learn that his place is walking at your side with his head at about your left knee. The controls for this are the leash, the choke collar, and the command HEEL. You'll see later (page 120) how a pup is trained to heel and not to bolt ahead or lag. He'll learn by trial and error that it's more comfortable to walk with a slack leash. It's so easy to be a gentleman.

THE OUTSIDE TURN

Once the pup learns to walk straight ahead with you, it's simple to teach him to follow no matter which way you turn. Turns should be started with the left leg, the leg nearest to him. He will learn to follow that leg because it is the easier one for him to see. By patting your left leg you get his attention and signal him that something is going to be taking place. Then you start the turn. As you can see in the pictures the trainer is using body English to "help" the dog around. By leaning over a little you are also showing the dog that he is doing well, since that bent position is not a threatening one to the dog. He will have learned earlier that he has to speed up a little in order to get around and still stay in position. This is where the choke collar becomes useful.

The trained dog will do this turn very well and we'll show you later how the pup learns it. The important thing here for you, the trainer, is to see how the professional trainer does it. He helps the dog around with the slap on the leg and the "body English"—but even those things are eliminated later, and the dog will learn to follow your left leg.

The inside turn is more difficult for the dog. It should not be taught until the outside turn has been mastered. The dog must follow the inside leg. As a pup, as you will see, he'll get all tangled up in your legs. What you do, until he learns this command, is to cut him off as he goes around . . . pushing him out of the way as you go. He soon gets the idea that it's better for him to follow than lead.

THE INSIDE TURN

The inside turn may confuse a small pup the first time or so that you try it, but he'll get it fast if he's paying attention. While the trainer is walking he gives the signal that something is going to happen. Some trainers call the dog by name in order to get his attention. The slapping of the leg is better because it does two things . . . gets his attention and focuses it on the legs. As you see in the sequence of pictures, the left leg starts the turn, but it's the right leg that blocks the forward direction of the dog. Here the dog has to slow up and let you get around him. This is the exact opposite of the outside turn. You can see how this is taught. The dog won't like being bumped, so he'll learn to slow up for his own comfort.

The retriever works from the sit position. He's looked and gotten the direction . . .

SIT . . . ON YOUR FOUNDATION . . .
IS THE FOUNDATION

The SIT command is the basis of training. This is the command that gives the trainer control over all situations and the opportunity to move about and set up the next lesson. Training a dog is like building with blocks. The SIT command is the foundation. All other commands stem from it.

A dog who will sit on command is a controlled dog. If the dog is doing or about to do something you do not want, the command SIT will either stop what is happening or prevent it from happening. For instance, if you are waiting for an elevator and another dog comes by, the command SIT will at least control your dog. Teachers seem to get better results with kids when they see trouble coming by having the kids do something constructive instead of constantly saying "no." The same thing works with a dog. If a dog gets excited when guests arrive at your door, it's better to have him obey the command SIT than to command NO. Besides, NO in that situation is not what you really want. You don't want him not to greet the guests; you want him to have a little dignity. The guests will make a fuss over him if he is well behaved, so that's his reward.

When teaching the commands, SIT must be learned first. It gets the attention and anchors him to a spot.

With the dog sitting, the trainer then can go about teaching STAY. It would be hard to teach STAY with the dog in the standing position or walking around. The trainer has control because the sitting dog has to make a deliberate motion to get up to break the STAY command. If you have fast reflexes you can stop him as he prepares to get up . . . that's how he is going to learn what the word "stay"

. . . now, at the command to go, he's off running. SIT is the control in training.

means. The sitting position allows the trainer to move about to teach other commands also. To teach COME the trainer has to physically be away from the dog. He has the dog sit; then he can move away and teach the command COME.

Retrievers are some of the most precisely trained workers. They take all their commands from a sitting position, whether it be at the handler's side or a hundred yards away. On whistle command, no matter where he is, the dog will stop, turn, sit, and wait for his next command signal. If he is swimming he'll do the next best thing to sitting when he hears the whistle . . . he'll turn and tread water and look at his handler and wait for his next command. This shows how important this command is. A dog must obey it faultlessly, no matter what he is doing. It's the control for everything that follows. SIT is the attention-getting command. When the dog is commanded to sit it's natural for him to pay attention to you. He'll be "all ears" . . . either he'll want to be released from the command so he can get back to the thing he was doing, or he'll get to learn that another command is going to follow. It's the command that changes the subject without his realizing it.

Teaching a dog to sit is not difficult. The difficult part is teaching the trainer that he must always insist on obedience from the dog. If you give the command and the dog, no matter what age, learns that you won't make him obey, he'll always look for a crack in your armor. He'll start to respond reluctantly, hoping you'll forget about it. He'll do it in his own sweet time if you let him get away with it. The command is SIT, so let him know that you want action . . . from the top to the bottom.

SIT is taught from the walking position with a grown dog. You use your hands to . .

SIT . . . HOW TO TEACH IT

It seems a shame to have such a well-trained fellow as this Labrador go through this kindergarten lesson for the pictures. He doesn't need all the handling; he'll do this command on voice or whistle. One blast of the whistle means the same to him as the voice command SIT. But he's helping out and is showing what he went through to learn his lessons as a pup.

He is walked at the handler's left side, and when the command is given the handler's right hand lifts the dog's head by pressure with the leash. The handler's left hand simultaneously reaches back and pushes down on the dog's rump. He's pressured all the way down to the ground and held there. Then he's praised. Note how high the choke collar is worn. This is the correct positioning . . . just behind the ears.

It'll only take a couple of days for a dog to learn what this pressure means. Shortly you will see that on giving the command and raising the leash to get his head up, all you'll have to do is touch his rump and he'll go down. When he does it without the touch on the rump you'll be able to use less and less pressure lifting his head. Finally he'll do it on the voice alone. Once he has learned on leash, you can start him off the leash. If he doesn't respond instantly, put him back on.

If you wonder how a retriever learns to sit on one whistle blast, whether the dog is at the handler's side or a hundred yards away, it's simple logic. When he was first taught, as a ten-week-old pup, the voice command SIT was always followed immediately by one blast of the whistle. He came to associate both sounds with the command SIT, and he'll now do it on either one . . . voice or whistle. This is taught first by the handler's side, on leash. Then it's taught off leash. What is the control? A dog will try you off leash and think your control is gone. Not so.

78

. . . "tell" him what you want. Note how the leash is held to pull his head up as . . .

. . . the bottom goes down. The voice command is SIT. Then comes the praise for him.

On the first sign of reluctance put him back on leash, even if it means chasing him down. Then be damn firm and start the lesson over, but before it starts, give a corrective jerk on the collar. Then in a normal voice proceed. This teaches him that you are the boss and have ways of making him do what is expected no matter where he is . . . and I mean right now!

79

STAY . . . WATCH THE HAND . . . STAY

A finished dog should stay until the command is given to release him. There are many situations—on the street or in the home—when it is important to keep the dog out of the way.

After the dog sits on command, the left hand is held in front of his face as the command STAY is given. Then the handler walks forward slowly. It's important to note here that the handler's movements must be slow or the dog will think he's supposed to walk at his side as he steps off. The handler turns his hand over and gives the traffic cop's signal for "stop" and the command STAY is repeated. The command is sharply given with every step the handler takes. Then the trainer steps backward to the end of the six-foot leash. If the dog breaks from his position at any time, the whole procedure must be started from the beginning . . . from the sit position.

After he's learned STAY very well, test him to make sure he understands that he's to obey the voice and the "stop" hand signal; try to make him disobey by putting pressure on the leash with the right hand. In these pictures it would seem that this pup would rather have his head pulled off than disobey.

Finally, from this place in front of the dog, walk around him. Go all the way around giving the hand signal and the voice command. He should stay until released . . . if not, start over.

The STAY command is important not only for your convenience, it can save a pup's life. One day my daughter Gretchen was walking a new pup at heel. He had learned the command well, and it was now time to work him off leash. He spotted me across the street and bolted. He was on a collision course with a truck when Gretchen screamed "Sit! Stay!" Fortunately, the pup obeyed.

We'll have some more to say about teaching SIT . . . STAY in Chapter 8.

A well-trained dog will sit and stay put until he is released. The hand is used to reinforce the verbal command and the dog will learn to respond to either signal. Your walking around should make no difference to the dog. Many dogs will learn the command STAY, but as soon as the trainer moves they think it's also their signal to move. Keep putting the dog back in his spot until he gets the idea. When he has it you'll be able to put pressure on his collar and he still won't come until he gets the new command to do so.

DOWN . . . A COUPLE OF WAYS OF GETTING
THERE . . . BUT STAY

The command DOWN is in many ways an optional one to teach. Many handlers consider that the sit position provides enough control and lets the dog decide whether he wants to be sitting or lying. Many hunters do not burden the dog with this extra command. Around the house, however, it's good to have this additional control over the dog because in a social situation it gets the dog out of the way.

There are a number of methods to teach the command DOWN, and the size of the dog will have some bearing on which method you use. They all start the same way: the dog is put in the sitting position. Again, the hand is used as a signal. The palm is moved down as the command DOWN is given. The voice should say what the word is saying . . . DDDOWWnnn. The inflection is on the first part of the word, and the sound drops down with the hand.

The hand is used to show the dog what the voice command DOWN is. Note that in working with this dog the trainer has the leash on at all times. The leash gets to mean control. If the dog does not understand this command from the voice and hand, there are other ways to make the point.

OTHER WAYS TO TEACH DOWN

The command DOWN is taught with the dog sitting at your side. It's simple to teach to a small pup: after you give the verbal command and the hand signal you lean over and carefully lift his front paws and extend his legs. He'll then be down and you can even hold him while repeating DDDOWWnnn. With a grown dog, size will determine the method you choose. The two most common methods are to put a down pressure on the collar, as shown in the top pictures, or the dog can be rolled over on his side, as seen in the bottom pictures. There is another

In teaching DOWN, big dogs may have to be pulled down by applying pressure on the leash. Small dogs can be rolled on their side.

method for very big dogs. The leash is slipped under the trainer's foot to give him added leverage. Even a small person can handle a big dog this way. Pull up on the leash, and the choke collar will tighten and bring him down. It's better, of course, to start the training earlier with a puppy. He'll know all these commands before he gets big and harder to handle.

The SIT position will be more comfortable for your dog for a long period than the DOWN position, but he doesn't know that when the command is given. Lying on command is not as natural for the dog as sitting. It usually takes longer to get the DOWN command across to a dog, but often it's the trainer's fault. For some reason handlers confuse and misuse the command DOWN with the general corrective command NO. When a dog jumps up on someone it's wrong to command DOWN. It should be NO. This misuse causes confusion. A dog stealing food from the table hears the command DOWN . . . again it should be NO. DOWN should mean "Lie down," not "Stop what you are doing." Otherwise, when you teach the command to lie down, it's going to be difficult for the dog to understand your real meaning. There is another unfortunate thing about this command DOWN. Often it's used as a reprimand or to get the dog out of the way, and he can sense that.

Big dogs who don't get the idea may need real pressure. The leash under the foot will do the job. Command DOWN and pull up on the leash . . . he'll stay there.

The proof of the pudding. Now he's ready to do it off lead.

DOWN-STAY . . . AND STAY DOWN

To teach the dog to stay down, while you're at his side, the leash can be slipped under your foot, and if he goes to get up he can be quietly told to DOWN-STAY. A little pressure will keep him in place.

To test the DOWN command in a finished dog, use the same method we employed in the SIT command: walk to the end of the leash and tug it slowly while saying DOWN-STAY. When you leave the dog's side, as shown in the pictures, move very slowly and repeat the command DOWN-STAY often. When you get to the end of the leash and turn toward him, repeat the command DOWN and be ready to spring at him if he starts to break. This is where rapid motion is necessary. If he goes to get up, your springing movement will surprise him, and he'll get back down.

Once he learns this on leash you can start to train him to do it off. The verbal command DOWN-STAY should be enough, but trainers like to do it by hand signal also. It's good to have this refinement. If you have guests and the dog has been told to stay in his place but he decides that it's been long enough . . . a hand signal will hold him, and you won't interrupt the conversation with your guests to get your point across to the dog. The signal is the traffic cop's "stop" hand-signal: fingers together, palm facing him, then hand lowered toward the ground to show him what is wanted. This is taught by having the dog SIT . . . STAY, with you at the end of the leash. Give the DOWN verbally and simultaneously show the hand command. He'll soon get the point that either command means DOWN and stay there. Have patience with this command, he'll have learned SIT-STAY a lot faster. Teaching DOWN and DOWN-STAY takes time.

COME . . . THE COMMAND THAT MUST BE OBEYED

Any dog that understands and will obey the five words SIT, STAY, COME, HEEL, and NO is a controlled dog. The procedure for teaching the COME command is to add one more block onto the command SIT-STAY. With the six-foot leash and choke collar on the dog, the trainer walks to the end of the leash and turns facing the dog. The command COME is given while standing at your full height. Then, as you deliver the command, you lean over. The reason for the change of your position is to show the dog that you are friendly. Sign language, as we have said, is very important to the dog; standing over him in an erect stance is a threat to a dog . . . bending over demonstrates friendship.

The leash is used to teach the dog unconsciously that you are in control. If he won't come, he can be gently pulled toward you. If that is necessary, much praise should be heaped on him so he will learn that COME means good things. Most handlers get into trouble on this command because they lose their cool. If you try to shout the dog in, you'll only drive him away. But the biggest error is getting this command mixed up with NO. If the dog is doing wrong and you command COME, then you reprimand him for what he was doing and don't praise him for following your directions by coming, you are going to have a confused pup. If the dog needs reprimanding, go to him to do it . . . you will avoid the confusion. Don't ever ignore a dog when he has obeyed this command, even if you only say, "Good boy." Never at any time let him get away with not obeying. If he learns that you will forget the whole thing if he responds in his own sweet time, you'll have a dog that will obey only when he wants to.

Many people use a whistle for this command. The silent dog whistle is very good in the city because it won't disturb anyone. Many working dogs are trained to respond to the whistle because shouting loud enough is too difficult and in a wind the voice won't carry. The retrieving dogs need a whistle because while they swim they often can't hear the voice.

The whistle command to come is a trilling sound, not a blast. It's a fast "beep, beep, beep, beep." It almost invites the dog in. It's taught at the same time that the voice command is taught. As soon as the command COME is given, the handler should start the trilling and continue it the whole time the dog is coming to him.

It always amazes people to see a close-working hunting bird dog in action. They wonder how the hunter trains his dog not to run hundreds of yards ahead in a big open field. A dog can be trained for that in a city park. From the day he starts walking with the dog, the trainer never allows the dog to get too far ahead, even on their Sunday afternoon walks. When the dog does get too far he's brought back by whistle. By the whistle command COME the dog will learn his allowed distance and will stay just that far ahead of the trainer. If you watch a good close hunting dog work, you will see that every so often he'll glance back to see if he's about the right distance from the hunter. Some dogs will get so good at this that the whistle can be thrown away. Such a dog will be cast off to hunt, and if the hunter does not look at the dog, but looks away each time the dog glances back to check, the dog will continue about his hunting business. If the hunter stops walking and looks at the dog when the dog checks back, the dog gets to know something is wrong and will start to come in to find what the trouble is. The hunter, on walking again and dropping his eyes, is giving the dog the signal that all is well, and the dog will turn and continue his hunting. To accomplish this in a dog takes consistency in the training until it becomes a habit for him.

A young dog can read from your stance. He comes slowly . . .

. . . squat down and he recognizes a friendly attitude . . .

. . . he'll come a running and very happily greet you.

Note how the professional trainer "talks" to the dog with his body.

COME . . . THE STARTING METHOD

From the sitting position you can teach him the command COME with ease. If the dog doesn't respond immediately to the voice, jiggle the choke collar with the leash. He'll get up and come. If need be, bring him in by leash, but there is no need to be rough. Remember, you want him to like coming to you. Make your voice sound inviting . . . you want him to come. Give him encouragement to see what fun this is. With pups you can often teach this by turning and running away. The pup wants to be with you, so he'll come. Make it fun. Once the pup understands what you want when you command COME when he is in the sitting position, you can start to give the command when he is walking or playing. We start this command in the sitting position so the handler will have the necessary control.

SPRING THE COMMANDS ON HIM

A dog soon gets to know where the classroom is, and that he'd better obey in class or the teacher will use the rod. Therefore, once the commands are learned in the control situation they should be sprung on the dog at any odd moment . . . in the living room, in the park while playing, walking on the street. By doing this you are making learning a game. Dog trainers agree that dogs get a lot of satisfaction out of doing their thing, just as people do. And both people and animals like a lot of praise after they do what is being asked of them.

MAKING THE DOG A BELIEVER

Making the dog a believer in you is not only important in the COME command; it is also a basic part of all training. We've mentioned above that you should never reprimand a dog for something he has done wrong by calling him to you and then giving him what-for. He won't know if he's being scolded for what he did wrong or for coming to you as commanded. If you do reprimand him in this way, you should be able to understand why he comes reluctantly the next time you call him.

A working retriever is an example of a true believer. But even he must be taught this from the very beginning. These dogs have been bred for centuries to carry things in their mouths. That is their great pleasure in life. You never have to pat a retriever who loves his work and say, "Good boy." His reward is the retrieve. To teach such a dog to be a believer you must make sure that when you give him a command to retrieve there will always be something there, such as a dummy, for him to pick up. He'll learn then that if he follows your commands he'll find the thing he is to carry to you. He comes to understand that you know better than he does where the object is . . . he becomes a believer. He believes the object is there because you have told him so.

How does this apply to a house pet? Make him a believer too. The COME command is the best way to instill this faith. When you call him, make sure that you are pleased that he has done what you wanted. His reward will be a good pat and some special attention. He'll be a believer if you are a good guy to work for and always go out of your way to show it.

One way to make a dog a believer in you is to give him lots of praise when he's good. He won't mind harsh talk when he knows he is not pleasing you.

7. PROOF OF THE PUDDING

When I took my first course in chemistry in college I had a professor I'll always remember. Although I've forgotten a lot of the chemistry because I haven't used it in so long, he had a teaching method that has stuck with me. About the third or fourth lecture he stopped and said, "OK, you can put down your note pads and watch me. I want to try to show you what chemistry is." He then proceeded with some fascinating experiments. There was no doubt that he was a showman, but even more important, he was a skillful teacher. What he did was to show us what the end product of chemistry was, what we'd be able to do, before we laboriously learned all the details. Most teachers start at the beginning of a subject and build step by step until the final product is reached. That is sound thinking, but many a student gets lost along the way because he doesn't have a perspective.

I've tried to show you, by following a professional trainer at work, how you must operate as a trainer. Now, taking a leaf from my professor's book, I'd like to show you some proof of the effectiveness of the early training method.

Dogs that guide the blind have a responsibility in life that very few people ever have. The safety of their masters depends upon them. One misstep could mean disaster. These dogs are trained to handle complicated city problems. Your dog will never be called on for such duty, but there is much to learn from the guide dog training that will help you understand how to handle your dog. Theirs is a proven method, and you'll train your pup in much the same way.

It takes only thirteen weeks, from start to finish, to take a raw dog and turn him into a guide dog. When you see him on the street working, you marvel at his performance. It took you years in college to learn your profession. How can they train a dog so thoroughly in a matter of weeks?

The trainers of these guide dogs for the blind have no secrets; there is no magic in what they do. It's logical step-by-step, one-thing-at-a-time training. The story of their success does not begin with the year-old dog that they train to completion by the time he's fifteen months old. They start back at the beginning.

In most cases guide dog trainers breed their own stock. They consider the temperament of the breed and that of the individual dogs and bitches. Although German shepherds have been used traditionally for this work, more and more they are being replaced by Labrador and golden retrievers because of their reliability. Of course, small dogs can't be used because the dog has to be tall enough for the sightless person to work the harness, and the dog must be strong enough to pull out and lead his master.

Trainers for guide dogs go to a lot of expense and effort to get the best breeding they can. We have given you ways of selecting the breed you want and of choosing the best pup from the litter. Let's assume your dog comes from a litter as well bred as the guide dogs; the starting points are the same for both of you.

In both cases the litter is left together until the pups are seven weeks of age, old enough to be weaned. In the next stage the amateur trainer has an advantage over the guide dog trainer, since he gets into the act as trainer during the fourth critical period in the pup's mental development. This is impossible for the guide dog trainers; it would take a tremendous staff to give the number of pups they handle each year the individual attention they must have.

Therefore, they do the next best thing. Seven-week-old pups are put out into foster homes for a year. This has become a major project of the Department of Agriculture's 4-H Clubs for young people all over the country. Socialization and early training at this specific age are considered so important that whole staffs do nothing but place the pups and train the 4-H youngsters in handling them.

The dog learns to deal with people and things at this age when it is so important. He also learns his SIT, STAY, and COME commands. He's given security so that no fears develop. Housebreaking is taught, and the pup is expected to be a good member of the family. He lives with the family, goes shopping with them, plays with them, and does all the things that your dog will do with you. They do put certain restrictions on the young trainer. The pup is not taught to heel because that will only have to be unlearned when the dog goes back for his guide training. The puppy is never allowed to cross the street diagonally since this is something he is never permitted to do when he becomes a guide dog.

What kind of animal do the guide dog trainers want back when the year is up? They want a dog who has made his bond with humans very strong. They want a pup who enjoys learning and who is temperamentally dependable.

Jeff Lock, expert with the Guiding Eyes for the Blind organization in Yorktown Heights, New York, firmly believes that it's necessary to start with a sound, well-bred dog, but that the environment he's reared in is just as important. A kennel-raised dog will not be suitable for training. His ways get set, and he can't put up with stresses that exist outside in the world. In spite of his training and conditioning, a dog under stress will always revert to his fears. So it's important that the breeding be good and the environment be controlled to eliminate as early as possible those things that will create the fears. Mr. Lock gives as an example subway gratings on the sidewalk. If a dog doesn't learn at an early age that they really won't hurt him, he can develop such a strong fear of them that no matter how much conditioning he gets, he reverts to that fear reaction.

Trainers for the guide dogs agree that the 4-H Club holding system is the best answer to a very practical problem, but they could do so much more if it were physically possible to start the dog with the trainer and the blind person from that early age. As it is, when the dog comes back to the school at his physically mature age, his environment is changed, and the trainers start from the beginning and reinforce the basic commands all over again.

Teaching a prospective guide dog to stop at curbs is typical of the training he gets. When the dog is walked on lead he is given a mild jerk on the collar when he approaches the curb, and then he is expected to sit. Some dogs become apprehensive about curbs. In such cases the trainer will start over with the dog and deliberately walk over the curb without stopping. Thus he shows the dog that there is nothing to fear about the curb situation. After running the curbs for a while the dog will be started again with the mild jerk when he comes to a curb. The dog gets conditioned to stopping without unnecessary unpleasantness. This kind of training is using animal sense. Any good city dog should learn to stop before crossing the street.

While walking a dog, as the trainer approaches the curb he slows down. This becomes a signal to the dog. As the trainer gets to the curb, he stops and commands "Sit." Then he waits for the traffic to clear. As he steps off the curb, he commands "Heel." He's careful to step off with the same leg each time—with the left leg if the dog is heeled on that side. Dogs can't read traffic lights, so to be consistent one must stop at the curb and go through this training even if the light is green. It's a question not of training the dog to walk with the pedestrian traffic but of teaching him not to go off the sidewalk without stopping. If he's trained to stop he'll never get into trouble. The bolting dog is the one that gets killed by cars.

By the end of the three months the dog will have been trained to handle traffic; the clearances of spaces, so that he and the blind person will be able to pass and not bump into things; and getting on and off elevators, trains, and subways. For a country dog, raised on the farm of a 4-H Club family, he does pretty well learning to navigate in department stores . . . revolving doors and all!

A dog that begins living in the city at seven weeks is of course introduced much earlier to all the things that produce stress for a city dog. He'll become used to these things at such an early age that he won't have fears of them. As one guide dog trainer put it, "I wish there were 4-H Clubs for city kids. Then dogs would be acclimated to the city sooner." The pup's environment and early contact with humans are basic necessities for producing a dog that can take this rigorous training.

If the teenage boys and girls of the 4-H Clubs can achieve the results they do, other teenagers and adults should be no less capable of training a pup!

This is one of the pups that was tested back in the section on picking the right dog for you from the litter. He will be getting his early training from one of the 4-H club children who prepare the dogs for the rigorous training that is yet to come. The pup arrived at his temporary home at the age of seven weeks.

INTELLIGENCE AND
TRAINABILITY . . .
START EARLY

People who think that various breeds have differing intelligence don't know what they are talking about. Experiments by animal behaviorists, as we have seen, have proven that no one breed of dog is more intelligent than another. They have proven, contrary to what many think, that after making allowances for size, agility, stamina, and so on, all litters are very similar. They all start out the same. Scientists say that a mature dog's intelligence is influenced by its emotional make-up and its early experiences. They have found that any differences in the intelligence test results of adult dogs stem from the way they have been reared and trained. We seem to confuse trainability with intelligence.

The guide dogs are an example of this relationship. The high percentage of success with these dogs is due, as we have seen, to the careful early handling and training. A dog that has had a wide range of experiences during the formative period will be motivated and will be able to accept a lot of training. A dog that has not had good early experiences will try to stay in a self-restricting environment. He'll shy away from new things and will never learn, but this will have nothing to do with his intelligence. He may seem stupid, but the real stupidity is on the part of the people who handled him at an early age.

Because of their early experiences, guide dogs for the blind, when they leave their foster homes to begin their final training, are unafraid, full of curiosity, and eager to learn.

SIT, STAY, COME are learned and repeated. Schooling is a big part of each day . .

. . . START EARLY

The obvious purpose of getting the dog into a 4-H home is to socialize him and lay a foundation for the important work to come. A simple thing like car rides, mild restrictions and simple schooling will make a pattern for a way life. Control the environment and the dog will get no "hang ups." Breaking bad habits is something not even the professional wants to deal with.

Restrictions and learning his place are part of getting him ready to lead the blind.

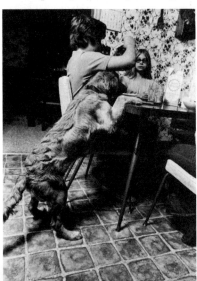

oup has to learn to learn and like it.

Having a job is important, and they both have one, but there is always time out for fun.

Our golden retriever pup, now a year old, is brought from the 4-H home and is ready to take training for the full responsibility of a blind person. Turn the page to see just how fast he learns and the concepts he has to master.

A guide dog has to stop at curbs. As they approach, the trainer must communicate to the dog that of all the things around, it's the curb to be aware of, so he . . .

GUIDE DOGS LEARN TO STOP AT A CURB

In spite of his remarkable accomplishments, the guide dog is not a superdog. That early training and socializing makes learning his way of life. Here is a pup that learns to stop at a curb on command. The curb is patted when the dog stops and sits. Then the dog is praised. This is repeated until the dog learns that it is at the curb that the trainer wants him to stop. It's this kind of animal sense on the trainer's part that you have to learn. There will be no reason why you couldn't teach this to your dog. This pup will learn it—and not fail—in two to three weeks. You don't have to rush that fast. If you start early the dog will learn this habit as you go on your daily walks.

. . . taps the curb repeatedly with his foot and commands the dog to stop. This is repeated and then the trainer bends over and taps the curb with his hand. Soon the voice command means "Stop at curb," and then the curb itself means "Stop."

Here is the first attempt. The dog seems completely oblivious to the approaching car . .

CARS . . . TRAFFIC . . . KEEP YOUR DISTANCE

As an example of this, notice how quickly the pup in these photos learned what was expected of him. His trainer was walking as a blind person would. The approaching car was a set-up. The dog was walked on a course that would have led to a collision with the car. He seemed to be paying no attention. When the car and dog were about to collide, the trainer slapped the car and made a loud noise. Then his hand continued down and struck the dog. A firm NO command was given. It took only one such experience to show the dog what was expected. On the next pass of the car, the dog stopped. These pictures were actually the first and second times the dog was put to the test. This was repeated over and over to reinforce the lesson, since this is an area where the dog mustn't fail.

The very next time the dog paid attention and stopped. That's pretty fast learning. He . . .

At the danger point the trainer strikes the passing car with a loud bang and then hits . . .

The lesson here for the amateur trainer is that a dog will become as reliable as any industrious person but the training has to be consistent. The guide dog trainers never deviate from their planned program, knowing that the dog, like a child, learns by habit.

. . . the dog, giving him a good scare. The dog recoils in fear . . . a lesson learned.

aited until the danger passed and then proceeded. This will be repeated until it's automatic.

Obviously the dog can get under but a blind person couldn't . . .

HOW HIGH IS HIGH?

The accompanying photos provide one more demonstration with a guide dog to show how far you go in training a dog. Here the abstract concept of height is taught with the same training methods that are used to teach such simple basic commands as SIT and STAY. It all boils down to putting a dog into a situation, and with correction and praise he will learn what you want him to do. Obviously, a blind person can't get through places a dog can, so a guide dog must be taught the concept of space. Here is a demonstration of the first lesson. This pup was started with a low barrier. As you see, he learned on the second try not to go under it. As his training continues, higher and higher obstacles will be used. Eventually, by repetition he'll learn what he's allowed to pass and when he must stop. There is no magic here . . . it's all conditioning. You won't be teaching your dog such difficult space concepts, but it will help to sharpen your animal sense when you realize that it can be done.

On the second try he already got the point. On approaching he stopped and looked up . . .

4

5

2

. . . the board is banged, dog slapped and scolded for going . . .

3

. . . under. The barrier is pointed out and it's a no no.

. . for instructions. The way to go on was around the obstacle. He learned a space concept!

6

7

Sam

8. AN AMATEUR TRAINER

In the last chapter we saw the professional dog trainer at work and tried to demonstrate how important it is to start the training early. Obviously the guide dog organizations wouldn't go to the trouble and expense of placing their young dogs in foster homes with young people unless they considered it vital to the training.

Now let's turn to a typical situation of an amateur training a dog for the first time. This is an actual, real-life case history, not specifically set up for this book. Mary and her pup Sam, a German shepherd, did not come together on his forty-ninth day, as we advocate. All the same, there is much to learn from their example. You will see a lot of very good training being done by Mary. She was a natural: consistent, firm, and compassionate. Sam proved to be a fine pup. He worked hard and enjoyed the training. You could tell that he loved Mary, but he received a few scars, and we don't know what his situation was in those important weeks before he came to live with her.

THE SHORT STORY OF SAM

Sam came into Mary's life because of a near tragedy. Mary runs her own business in town and has her own offices. One day she was robbed at knife point by two young punks who entered her office. They didn't harm her, but although the things they stole were of little value, the experience was traumatic. Mary's husband suggested better security measures for the office and a dog capable of protecting her. Although she had little or no experience in training, she decided it was a good idea. She went to a pet store and bought Sam. She wasn't sure of his breeding or his exact age, but he was an alert smart pup . . . and home they went together. Mary sought the advice of a professional dog trainer and then contracted with him to teach her to train and finish Sam off as an attack dog.

The plan was that Mary would bring her dog to work every day. He would stay with her in her office, then each night her husband would drive from his office and pick both of them up and they'd go home. Each day the trainer would arrive, and they'd have a training session during lunch time.

I happened into this picture when I met Mary and Sam during one of their walks; my office was down the street. I explained to Mary that I was writing this book and asked if she would mind if Sam was included in it. That's how it came about that we all started working together.

In educating Sam, Mary did have some help from the professional dog trainer, and in this case it finally led to trouble. From the experimental work of the animal behaviorists, we know that dogs who have absolutely no human contact or training during the fourth and fifth critical periods are practically untrainable. Sam was an example of a pup who fell somewhere in between and was handled one hour a day by a trainer who really didn't understand how to deal with such a young animal. Sam was about twelve weeks old when he was bought at a pet shop. Nothing was known about his background, and his birthday was just a guess on the part of the pet store clerk.

Love at first sight brought Mary and Sam together.

Since Mary had never trained a dog before, she hired the trainer to help her. Unfortunately, the trainer knew nothing about a dog's early mental development and less than he should have known about teaching step by step. He may have been great with older dogs, but he finally produced confusion in Sam by starting right off in the role of the dominant trainer. Sam spent one hour each day with the trainer, but during that hour he was supposed to learn, by being shook up if need be, that a dog's role was to obey, and there would be no nonsense about it. The trainer's method was to speak and act in a rough manner and immediately change to a sweet loving tone. You could see that Sam was only trying to avoid the unpleasantness of the situations. Since he wasn't sure yet what was wanted, the abrupt change from the harsh to sweet treatment was confusing.

Luckily for Sam, he had to deal with the trainer for only one hour a day, and the rest of the time he was Mary's. He became devoted to her, and she didn't have it in her to be so dominant. Instead, she was firm and kind. You could see he was happy with her; his head was up, he was alert, and he learned his lessons from her as fast as any dog could.

Before we tell the end of the story, let's see in pictures the great progress Sam and Mary made together. The setting for many of the pictures is Mary's office. In the daytime that was Sam's home. They did all the right things together. This case history will show that if you recognize how important the pup's mental development is during this period, then use common sense and do not push or lag behind, the dog will do the rest . . . and the results will be spectacular and rewarding. If the seventh to sixteenth weeks are not handled correctly, however, problems will most likely develop.

CONFIDENCE AND TRUST ARE IMPORTANT

The first job in Sam's training was to take the place of the pup's mother. That was an easy way for Mary to gain his love and trust and for him to develop confidence in her. At the same time he began to learn that the strange, outlandish city things were not going to hurt him. In Mary's neighborhood the steam coming from the street manhole covers bothered Sam at first. The trainer should be aware of those things that might frighten his dog and plan to familiarize him with them as part of the training. At first a pup will balk. He is not sure, so the trainer shouldn't be unkind to him. He should speak in a soft voice and reassure the pup as he is put through the experience, which should be repeated until he accepts it as part of life.

LEARNING WITHOUT KNOWING IT

There are various ways a pup can learn his lessons. The first and most painless is learning without knowing it. For example, if a dog is walked on leash and never allowed on the right side of the trainer, after a while he will feel uncomfortable being on the right. If he's always on the left, almost without knowing it, he'll come to realize that is his place. Incidentally, a right-handed person will find it best to have a dog on his left. It keeps the dog out of the way and makes carrying packages or opening doors easier.

How did Sam learn about open doors and not to bolt through them? It wasn't by a formal lesson, and he learned it without knowing he was. He knew that the open door meant going out, and he liked that, so it was natural that he'd become excited and want to rush things a bit. Without any discomfort, Sam became a gentleman. When he rushed out ahead of Mary she closed the door on the leash behind him. Obviously, being in the hall alone with his leash held fast by the door was not what he wanted. He couldn't be upset with Mary about this. He did it to himself. It didn't take him very long to learn to wait and go out with Mary at heel. He figured out for himself that bolting ahead wasn't what he wanted.

A good trainer will work out in his own mind the things a dog has to learn that can be taught with this unconscious training method. It takes consistency on the part of the trainer to accomplish it.

Unconscious learning is accomplished by putting a dog in a situation and consistently directing the response you want. You give him no choice. A habit is established, and since there is no other way, the result is a learned pattern of action on the dog's part.

Mary didn't have to say a word to cure Sam of bolting ahead of her out the door. The first time she let him go, closed the door behind him, and he was trapped on the leash outside. Next time when she started to close it he acted like a gentleman.

LEARNING AND ENJOYING IT

Putting fun into the training will make it a lot easier on both pupil and teacher. There are many situations where it is necessary to use pressure. It is most important for your dog to learn as much as possible on the unconscious and fun levels. A pleasant method makes learning fun.

Don't think for one moment that a dog doesn't get a satisfaction out of an accomplishment. The little accomplishments are what makes the bond between man and dog strong. Because of his built-in desire to please, a pup enjoys his work. At first the bond was established because you took the place of his mother and fulfilled his needs. Work is the next step in cementing the bond.

Mary had a real job for Sam: acting as watchdog while she worked alone in her office. More will be said later about dogs for protection, but at this early age it's fun to teach a young pup to bark on command. This whole task has to be learned by association. There's no real language between man and dogs. It's easy to say to even a preschool-age child, "If the bell rings, or if you hear anyone coming up the hall, let Mommy know." But try that with a dog.

Mary wanted Sam to bark on a command that only the two of them knew— the sound made by clearing her throat. She set out to teach Sam to bark on this command by playing with him and using a tidbit as the reward if he made any sound. Sam must have questioned Mary's sanity as she went through her antics. By jumping about with the food in her hand and making the strange noise in her throat, her excitement finally aroused Sam, and in his exuberance, he stood up and made a squealing sound. He was given the tidbit. With more encouragement and a few tango steps, Mary finally got a bark out of him. She repeated her nonsense every hour or so, and she got him to respond with a bark to all her dancing. Next day she repeated it. Then that night at suppertime she prepared his meal and was now ready to make the transfer from his barking at her jumping around to his barking at the throat-clearing command alone. She cleared her throat so hard and so long, trying to get him to understand, that she lost her voice, but what was worse for Sam, he missed his supper. He didn't understand yet what she wanted. About 11 o'clock that night she decided to try again. This time, with the food dish in hand, Mary uttered a rather scratchy command and added a few dance steps to it. Sam, either from hunger or recognizing the dance step, let out a bark. Mary happily gave him his supper. The next morning he barked for breakfast on the first throat-clearing command alone. That fast, he got the point.

For the next week or so Sam had to answer the command with a bark before he got fed. During the day he got a tidbit and lots of praise for barking when Mary cleared her throat. Finally, the food reward was gradually removed, and Sam was barking on command and accepting praise as his reward. The command was sprung on him at strange times and places. He was to learn that he was to bark no matter what else might be happening. Mary's plan was gradually to diminish the loudness of her command. Sam was to bark on an almost inaudible noise from her throat.

STARTING AN ALARM DOG'S TRAINING

This is the first step in making Sam an alarm dog. He has to bark on command. At first the dog and the trainer will feel foolish, but the excitement will get a squeal out of him and that is the beginning. The tidbit will help, and before you know it he'll be barking on the secret command. It's like learning to bark for supper.

While this was happening, Mary had some more goodies for Sam to learn. He was taught that a knock at the door meant to bark. That was easy for Mary to teach. She did her little dance, cleared her throat, and knocked on the door all at the same time. Acting like a one-armed paper hanger, she got her point across, as you can see in the pictures. Then she did one more thing. She let Sam sleep by the door for part of each day. Without his knowing it, she was showing him that this was his territory. Since every dog has an innate drive to protect his area, she was starting him on the road of being her watchdog at an early age when he still loved and trusted everybody. Sam didn't have to understand then that he was being trained to protect Mary. All he was going to have to know, when he grew to

STEP TWO IN ALARM DOG TRAINING

The second step in making Sam an alarm dog is to teach him that the area near the door is his territory (upper left). Let him sleep and play near the door and when he's older he'll consider the place his. Teaching him to bark at a knock is easy. With the same procedure as on the last page, the excitement and the tidbit plus the knocking will teach him what you want him to do. In the right-hand picture, Mary is starting to get the results wanted. It took only a few weeks to have Sam bark at any time on the secret command. At this point it is still a fun game.

be a powerful dog with a deep bark, was that when Mary cleared her throat he was to sound off.

This training was an important part of Mary's plan of having a big dog in the city. Sam was well on the way to being her protector and he was only half-grown. This was all fun learning. Sam did miss one meal, or at least had it late, but that really will not hurt a dog.

Learning without knowing it and learning by fun, as we have seen, put no pressure on the dog. The dog is put into a situation, and he learns from that what is best for him and what the master wants. There are other situations that require a classroom approach, but even those don't have to be taught with the rod.

LEARNING AND DAMN WELL KNOWING
IT'S TO BE LEARNED

The commands SIT, STAY, and COME are not learned by unconscious or fun learning. They are "classroom" lessons. We have shown that a very young pup will learn simple commands if you repeatedly show him what you want. You should set up the class situation so he gets to learn that you are his teacher as well as his mother. He's not going to like the "classroom" as well as he liked the "schoolyard" where it was all play.

This third kind of learning will take some understanding on your part. It's necessary to make the class a distasteful experience. This is the area where Sam's professional trainer went wrong. His attitude was that roughness would show Sam what was wanted. You must show a dog with firmness what is wanted and do it in a controlled situation where he can't miss the point. There is a great difference between firmness and being shook up. Mary set up school each day in the hall. There were no distractions there so she could get Sam's undivided attention. Other animals, objects, or people will only distract a pup. Like a child, a pup will try to change the subject when he's put under stress. Your job is to teach him that the stress isn't so bad and that the learning is pleasant. You are not only teaching a command, you are teaching him that this formal lesson won't hurt him and that he might as well get used to it.

Professional trainers for the guide dogs say that the problem with most dogs is that their masters don't have animal sense . . . animal understanding. It will show up when these class lessons take place. If things are not going too well, the trainer must ask himself if the dog understands what is wanted. Loud talk or rough handling isn't going to make the dog get the point. Use your head: trying to have a pup learn a long SIT-STAY command isn't going to work very well if he hasn't completely learned the simple command STAY. A pup, like a child, has a short attention span and it must be considered in training, so don't ask a pup to sit and stay too long. Once you've learned his attention span, gradually increase the time.

It is really during these lessons that the dog gets to learn that you are the boss. He has learned a lot of things without even knowing it, but it's necessary to have these formal sessions for him to learn the responsibility of obeying you.

Learn to anticipate what the dog is going to do. For example, while teaching a pup to sit and stay, if you see he is going to break from the stay situation, quickly command COME. Now he has done two things right instead of one thing wrong. Now you can praise him instead of scolding him . . . that keeps the learning going. Later, when he is sure of the commands, you can gradually put the pressure on to do it your way. While he's learning, it's best to praise him even if he only stays a matter of seconds. Then you have him do it again, right away, and there is no stress in the learning situation.

Any quiet area can be set up as the classroom. Make sure there is enough space to work and that the teacher-pupil atmosphere is established each time you start the class. This in no way should be a threat to the dog, but it does mean business starts.

We go to the trouble of spelling out your role because most dogs that give trouble are the ones whose masters unfortunately are not understanding teachers. If there is any one thing that needs repeating it's that as a trainer you have to be consistent and firm, but not overbearing.

You have to expect that the dog will try you out. He'd like nothing better than having you do it his way. Even good kids in school will see how far they can go with a substitute teacher, hoping she'll relent and they'll play instead of work. The teacher who can take a little trying and laugh it off but at the same time make the kids work wins two points . . . one, she gets the lesson across, and two, she establishes who is boss.

The proper use of reprimand requires careful judgment. The dog's age is a very important consideration, as is whether you think he understands what is expected. In the fourth critical period there is no reprimand for failure to obey, but once the pup is twelve weeks old we expect him to obey the commands he has learned. Then the reprimand is to make him start over again if he gets stubborn. The voice gets sharper and the handling of the leash firmer, but there is no need to blow one's cool. If you are teaching STAY and he starts to COME, just walk him back to the beginning spot and start over with the command SIT. The tone of your voice should show that you are not pleased. It should be a controlled displeasure. Don't become angry and frighten the pup. Don't let him fool you with the hurt act. Many dogs learn to act shy or hurt, and that stops the lessons. Some pups will even roll over on their back to show that they are submissive and don't want you to teach those nasty commands. Such dogs will have to be joshed into playing the lessons game until they see that it isn't so bad, and in fact is pretty good, since they get a lot of praise when they do what is being asked. The strong-headed pup has to be controlled with voice and leash to make him understand you mean business. The important thing is to make the classroom part of every day's activity. The dog has to go to school and know that he's there. As one guide dog trainer put it, "Do it with love and respect but leave a little place in the training for the fear of the lord."

HOME IS WHERE THE MASTER IS

Let's look and see how well Sam and Mary did, although he missed those early crucial weeks when he should have been with Mary instead of in a cage in a pet shop. We can see what and how he learned.

During the day Sam's home was in Mary's office. A place was made for him under a table, where he wouldn't bother others and where they wouldn't bother him. The spot was draftless, and he had something soft to lie on. During the early stay in the new place the leash was kept on. He dragged it about. It was a simple irritation to remind him that life wasn't all easy, but it finally came to mean that he was under control. Actually he got so used to the leash that it became one of his playthings. At first the only learning required was to get used to the big new kennel.

OFFICEBREAKING

Housebreaking was nothing new to Sam. He'd learned that at the apartment; in the office he had to obey the same rules. Doing his business outside is much more natural for a dog. By taking the sheet of newspaper that was underneath the soiled sheets to street curb, the dog will learn quickly the association you wish him to make. It took Sam only a day to get the point, and he went for the curb as soon as he got out of the office.

The paper is the place! It won't take long for Sam to learn if he gets praise. Then the top sheets with scent . . .

. . . are taken to the street. It's made clear that it's for the same purpose as indoors. He'll get that fast and will learn to use the gutter. Don't let him use the sidewalk.

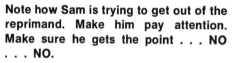
Note how Sam is trying to get out of the reprimand. Make him pay attention. Make sure he gets the point . . . NO . . . NO.

THE COMMAND IS NO!

In the fifth critical period the command NO becomes very important. Earlier we've used the command, but not harshly. Now it's time to make sure he really understands that NO is a command just like SIT, STAY, COME. Make sure your voice and gestures indicate that you've had enough of this nonsense and you'll have no more of that. This is where it's good to have the leash on the pup. He's been wearing it around the house, now it's your means of showing who is in control. Hold him up short and don't let him evade the issue. Without the leash he will try to get away from you. On the leash he'll look away to avoid this unpleasantness. Don't let him get away with that . . . make him look at you.

Incidentally, if a child is training the dog, be careful that he doesn't nag a pup with the NO command. Children have a way of taking out on a dog what teachers and parents do to them. A six- or eight-year-old child can accomplish a lot in the teacher's role, but he should be supervised. It's important with the NO command to be consistent. One of the ways to end up with an unruly dog . . . or for that matter, an unruly child . . . is to use the NO command sometimes and then let him get away with the same offense at other times. If a matter is considered a NO command offense, it should always be considered as such. Deviation on the trainer's part will cause confusion.

SIT-STAY . . . I MEAN IT

One of the best places to teach the command for a long stay is in the hallway of an apartment or a long, narrow yard. The corridor limits the "classroom" so that you have all the control you need. The leash is still used in this command because it means control to the dog. You place the pup at one end with the command SIT and then the command STAY. Now, you step backward away from the pup, and you command STAY with every step you make. At the same time you push your hand, giving the stay signal, toward him. When you get to the end of the leash you drop it and continue backward.

The first time Mary and Sam tried this there was trouble. Of course, Sam wasn't sure what was required of him. Hadn't he always been close to Mary? Now was she leaving him? Each time Mary dropped the leash on the floor and got a yard or two further away from Sam he broke and came to her. After a half-dozen tries, while I was taking the pictures, I suggested that I try it. On the first attempt I was able to get all the way down the hall and duck into the open door so Sam couldn't see me. He stayed alone for a split second in the hall. Then I popped out of the doorway commanding STAY and he did. With that we stopped the lessons for the day.

Actually we didn't stop because Sam had had enough. I wanted Mary to figure out why I'd been successful with the pup and she hadn't. We talked it over and she noted two things that I did that she didn't do. First, she realized her commands were not as sharp as mine and were not given with the authority needed to make them commands and not requests. The other thing she noted was that she moved too fast. At this stage a dog is not learning by voice alone, and this was a perfect demonstration for Mary to learn that fact . . . fast movements excite a dog.

The next day we tried it again. Mary worked out in her mind exactly how she was going to handle the situation. On the very first try it worked. After she dropped the leash on the floor, she stood there giving the command STAY with a strong sharp voice and reinforcing it each time with the hand signal. Then very slowly she continued stepping backward. Back, back, back, back she went, giving the command. At one point the pup looked as though he were going to break and come to her. She shouted STAY. Back she continued, step by step, until she got to the open door down the hall. Then Mary sharply commanded STAY and stepped sideways into the door. In a second she poked her head out the door and commanded STAY. Sam held his seat. Mary repeated this over and over. She stepped into sight and then retreated into the doorway. Sam wasn't ever sure when he was going to see her again. It all worked and Sam got the point. Then she released him; they had a fine meeting, and Mary told Sam what a good boy he was.

Mary's problem at first was that her commands sounded like requests.

SIT-STAY . . . I MEAN IT

She's down the hall . . .   **Pops in doorway . . .**   **out of sight . . .**

"SIT-STAY"   **STAY. Mary retreats . . .**   **Mary moves back slowly . . .**

They started over (above), and this time her voice was firm. Each time she stepped back she commanded STAY. Each step backward was slow. If she had moved fast, he would have gotten up to go with her. The leash is dropped gently and the command is repeated as she takes each retreating step. Down the hall she stepped into an open door for only a second. Out she popped. He learned to trust her. She wouldn't leave him there . . . or would she? Each day the time out of sight was increased. This was Sam's first try. He learned to sit and wait for her command to come.

Sam learns the command.

Pops out . . .   **all the way out . . .**

Sam had to learn right from the beginning to walk Mary's way. He'll find that to walk comfortably there is only one place . . . next to her left leg.

HEEL . . .
AND THE
EARLY WALKS

Heel is something a dog should do . . . not be. A dog that pulls and always wants to be out front is a pain in the neck. From the very beginning give *him* the pain in the neck. When you want him to heel at your side hold him up short on the leash and give the command HEEL. At the same time pat your leg. That will become his signal to heel so that eventually he'll do it on either voice command or the hand signal. If you teach the pup to heel during these early walks it'll become second nature to him, he will learn his place and it won't require any special training effort on your part. If for some reason it doesn't work, then you'll have to use the choke collar. The corrective jerk will soon teach him where he should be. When he pulls ahead, command HEEL and give a quick jerk and immediately release the chain. When he drops back praise him. On these early walks, if he is the kind that keeps walking in your way, don't break stride but gently bump him out of your way. Give the dog a chance to learn this command before you're too harsh or use the choke collar too vigorously. If he's not getting the message by the time he's four to five months old then start to be firm.

Don't try to heel him off leash until he's doing a good job on it. Carry the leash and choke collar with you and slap your leg with it every time you give the command. The first time he refuses the command put the choke collar on and show him you mean business . . . there is no need for him to be in your way or anybody else's.

Let the dog learn all about the interesting things around him. He's just as inquisitive as you are. Things he does not understand could frighten him.

People on the street are always a problem. They want to play with the nice pup. This is O.K. up to a point. You can't have the dog wanting to make the advance to people. It is really best to keep the dog to yourself. This is especially so if later you want the pup to be an alarm dog. After Sam was a few months old, Mary avoided this kind of friendliness.

I advised Mary to keep in mind that it's not just exercise that is required during a dog's first walks. The pup has a lot of inspecting to do. The more he sees the less he'll fear. Animals fear the unknown just as man does. Mary wisely tried to give the pup as many experiences as she could at an early age. When he learned that various things wouldn't hurt him his training went easier. One should be ready to give a dog some reassurance. Instead of just dragging him on, talk to him and show him that you're not afraid. Try to understand his position . . . this is all new to him. Even bicycles, trucks, cartons, and people are strange. Mary learned to let Sam take his time to become accustomed to such things. This is an important part of a pup's training.

STEPPING OFF THE CURB

Habit is the technique for training. Sam learns to stop at the curb and sit. This curb training is much like that for the guide dogs. We want the dog to get used to the traffic. There is a safe time to proceed. Mary's left leg will give the signal. He has to be ready to move right away or the choke collar will tighten. He's learning two things . . . about traffic and how to heel with precision. Note how he too learns to watch the traffic and Mary had to learn something too . . . her first step has to be with the left foot.

AN EXERCISE IN COMPLETE TRUST

Like most dogs, Sam found subway gratings so unnatural that he automatically shied away from them. Usually gratings can be avoided, but in this particular case the rest of the sidewalk was blocked off for repairs. A secure dog will learn that his master will not lead him into trouble, and here was a way for Mary to get Sam over a natural fear and to trust her. She walked him over the metal grille and he balked. Slowly she brought him along and then sat and petted him and showed him that it wasn't so bad after all. The dog at heel must learn that he follows no matter what! By repeating this each time they took a walk, Mary soon taught Sam that this was just another strange, but harmless aspect of the city.

This subway grating was the only place Mary could walk so it was a good time to teach Sam that it might be uncomfortable but that it wouldn't hurt him. A little love gets him over this problem.

Sam had to learn that Mary would never lead him into a situation that would hurt him. The steam frightened Sam but if Mary said it was O.K. he learned that it was. Mary was firm but gentle and then Sam got her praise . . . that was good.

RESTRICTIONS IN A REAL SITUATION

From almost the first day that a pup comes to live in the big new kennel he'll hear the word "No" used, but he must also be shown that he has to put up with certain restrictions. From the beginning we try to get him used to the idea that life is not a bed of roses. Being tied to a parking meter while Mary went into a store was Sam's first real opportunity to learn that he didn't always get his way and the best thing to do about it was to make the best of it.

Mary made some mistakes too . . . they both had to learn. Sam was tied to the meter. She reassured him before she left, but of course he didn't understand that. Then Sam wondered what had happened to Mary when she left him, so he decided to bark his head off to bring her back. He soon found out that barking wasn't the answer, and that's when he discovered Mary's mistake. He was able to get out into the street. Of course, he wouldn't know that was dangerous. For Sam the good part of all this was that he, without realizing it, was learning not to be afraid of strangers, carts, or the strange noises. The important thing for Mary here was not to have returned to him if he kept on barking. If she had, he would've gotten the idea that his barking brought her back. Then that would be another problem to correct.

By the next day, only the second time he was tied on the street, Sam learned to take it in his stride. Truck sounds and even trains going by did not faze him. It is important to introduce the pup at a young age to all he will encounter later, be it in or outside the home . . . he won't develop the shyness and fears that are so hard to handle later. The scientists call this *environmental enrichment*.

Here is a necessary restriction. Sam can't go into stores. It's good for him not to get his way always. He has to learn to make the best of any situation. Mary ties him to a meter and goes off. Sam wonders where she has gone. . . .

. . Sam barks his head off hoping she'll take pity and return to him. He soon gets . . .

. . . tired. Mary's mistake was to tie him so he could get into the street. He makes
a few friends, learns that barking won't bring Mary. Then comes reunion!

SAM LEARNS RIGHT TURN AND LEFT TURN

Mary soon found out that there is nothing more annoying than walking with a dog who thinks *he* is taking *you* for a walk. The question, who is walking whom, had better be settled at an early age or a big dog will have you all over the sidewalk and a small one will be tripping you up. On a crowded street this is important for you, the dog, and the other pedestrians. A dog has to learn to weave in and out just as you do, but the difference is that you are the one who will make the decisions as to when you'll zig and when you'll zag . . . the dog follows you.

To teach turning at heel, the dog is held short on the leash. For a left-sided heel the leash is held in the right hand. The left hand is used to slap your left thigh to get the dog's attention as you give the command HEEL. What you are doing is teaching the dog that there are two commands for heeling, the voice and the patting of your leg. If you consistently teach this with both commands, the dog will soon learn to respond to either one, separately. If you are walking with a friend it will not be necessary then to interrupt your conversation to give the dog his command. When you see a crowded pedestrian situation or an obstacle coming a pat on your leg will remind him to watch his step.

To start, Sam was told to sit. With Sam seated on her left, Mary patted her leg for attention and commanded HEEL. She waited until she was sure she had his attention and then stepped off. The first step should be with the leg closest to the dog. This pulled him up instantly. He didn't like that, but it didn't hurt him. He soon got the point, that he had to respond instantly or it would be uncomfortable for him. The pressure of the leash against the trainer's left leg keeps the dog in the desired position. If the step-off is made with the right leg the dog will be behind by a foot when he starts to walk.

If you walk a figure eight you will teach the dog both right and left turns. You can see in the pictures that Sam, on his left-hand turn, was trying to anticipate which way Mary was going to go. He had learned, on the right-hand turn, that he had to get all the way around Mary, and he was getting ready to do it when she fooled him and turned left . . . Sam had to stand still while Mary went around on the left turn.

This also taught Sam another important thing for street walking: when he was held on short leash he had to pay attention and remain under control. When the leash was let out he was free to sniff and be on his own.

Sam starts the turn outside by not paying attention. Mary pats her leg but he's not with it. Off she goes and it is a little rough on him but that's the way he's going to learn. You can tell by his movements that he's not sure what is expected. Mary guides him around. Practice makes perfect.

The inside turn is more difficult for a pup. They're clumsy enough themselves without having your feet in the way also. But note how fast Sam learned to pay attention to Mary's patting her leg. His ears are up and he seems to be trying. She guides him around and he's getting the idea. Mary has to remember to start off with that left leg.

SPRING THE COMMANDS ON HIM

Test the pup when he least expects it. This is a way of getting the commands across. It makes learning a habit that he'll enjoy. You can see Sam likes it.

AN ERROR IN TRAINING

Sam was a delightful pupil—eager, smart, and full of fun. Since I was on the scene not as the trainer but as a reporter, I couldn't interfere with the work of the professional trainer and Mary, his client. From the very beginning I saw problems develop. It finally cost Sam his life.

Since Mary didn't have Sam during his early critical days we didn't know if he had received handling at the specific time set down by the animal behaviorists, but every indication I could see showed that the dog had not. Sam and Mary, as the pictures show, were a very good team. On the last roll of pictures I took of Sam, Mary was walking him down the street, and she gave him the command to bark by clearing her throat. Sam, thinking this was a fun game, started to bark. Mary was so pleased with him.

The problem that I saw from the beginning was that Sam was too young for what the professional dog trainer was trying to do with him. I noted each day when the trainer arrived that the greeting Sam gave the trainer was a good one, but when they started to work Sam always looked over to Mary as much as to say, "Do I have to do this?" Sam would do what was required as best he could, but his tail wasn't up. Sam was learning and he'd often stop and look over at Mary when the trainer was trying to drive a point home. Sam was too young to have points driven home.

Sam and Mary lived together twenty-three hours a day, and their progress was remarkable. The twenty-fourth hour, that hour with the trainer, was too confusing for him. The trainer kept stressing that he was a stern master. He was going to get results . . . that was what he was paid to do. But now let me try to be as objective as possible so I can set the whole scene for what turned out to be Sam's last twenty-four hours.

The trainer was not an unkind person, in fact, just the opposite. He was a very nice person, but what I saw him do the last time he was with Sam convinced me that he didn't understand young dogs. Mary, as I've already said, was elated with her success with Sam.

Jake, Mary's husband, was on the fringe of all the training, and when they'd all get home at night he learned from Mary how to handle Sam. The last night that they were all together Sam and Jake had trouble. Instead of obeying when called, Sam ran and hid under the bed. That isn't uncommon; kids will do the same sort of thing. One thing led to another, and Sam refused to come out. Finally, in desperation, Jake went under after him. He wasn't about to be caught, so he ran around the apartment and then back under the bed. The upshot was that Sam became so frightened that he wouldn't eat and wouldn't settle down even for Mary. The next morning, when the trainer and I arrived at Mary's office, she told us the whole story. "It's just a very unfortunate thing," she said. "Jake loves Sam and we're sorry it happened." She went on to say that Sam was still upset and off feed.

Then the trainer made his first mistake. That was the morning when Sam was to have his toenails clipped. Sam was lifted onto a cleared desk, forced to lie down, and forcibly held while the nail clipper was used. It was a most traumatic situation for the pup. He was very frightened. After it was all over, the trainer said that a dog has to learn that a dog does what you want, when you want.

Then the trainer proceeded to train Sam on a leash. At this time Sam might have been in his fourteenth week of life. The lesson was in a command called "come for." This is very nice to see in a finished dog, but it isn't necessary to teach it to so young a dog. The dog was put in the SIT-STAY position facing the trainer. On command, he was to heel, but to do "come for" he must walk to the right-hand side of the trainer, then go around him and come to the heel position at the trainer's left. Sam could not seem to do it. He wanted to walk straight to the left side and turn and be at heel. It was the simplest and fastest way to the heel position. He was trying to cooperate, but the walking around part was not sinking in. You could see the dog get confused as the lesson went on. He stopped and looked at Mary on almost every try. His tail was down and he moved slower and slower. The more he tried the worse he did. The session then became a pulling match with the trainer jerking Sam around into the desired position. I became so infuriated with what I was seeing that I interrupted the lesson and asked Mary to take the dog and do a SIT-STAY lesson that I wanted to photograph. I had to "change the subject."

The trainer knew Sam was upset from the night before. He should have seen that the nail-clipping episode had the dog scared to death. That day ended with Sam a frightened, confused pup. The whole nail-cutting business should have been postponed, and the training for the day should have included only things the dog had already learned. There is a time in all learning when building confidence is more important than forging ahead.

That evening Jake picked up Mary and Sam and drove to their apartment. While Mary cooked supper, Jake took Sam for a walk. Still upset, Sam, who was off leash, would not come on the command. The command was repeated in a firm voice. Sam bolted and ran out of the park . . . he never saw the car that hit him.

What can be learned from this tragedy? It's most important to recognize the dog's attitude toward the training. A traumatic experience can leave a scar if it's followed by other tense situations. Sam flipped out. He was too young for the pressure the trainer was putting on him. Learning at this early age has to be in the form of play games. At this stage SIT, STAY, COME, and HEEL are fun commands; NO is the only one that should be taught with firmness. The results of these commands are not important. What is important is that the dog gets to like the learning. Later all sorts of refinements can be taught, and this may require pressure. There is no reason, however, to use physical force on a pup until he is six or eight months old. During the seventh to twelfth week the simple commands can be learned by just showing the dog what you want. From the twelfth to sixteenth week you make him do what you want, but do this by having him repeat the lesson until he has learned it. The voice during those first weeks should be more coaxing than commanding. The handling should all be very gentle. In the twelve-to-sixteen-week period the voice should be more businesslike, and the leash should be handled accordingly. Sam's trainer was using a spike collar (a choke collar which has prongs to hurt) on him before he was four months old.

Just as detrimental as the spike collar at this age was another type of confusion Sam had to put up with. The trainer really had two jobs, to train both Sam and Mary, but this was very confusing for the pup. Sam would be set in the SIT-STAY situation in the middle of the hall where the training was going on, and the trainer would then go to Mary and start to explain to her a point about training. In his explanation, often the commands would be used. On hearing the words "Come" or "Heel," Sam would react and start to obey. The trainer would jump at him for moving and reprimand him. Sam got a good shaking up for doing what he assumed was what the trainer wanted. The trainer missed an opportunity. He could have turned the whole scene into a reward situation. Wouldn't it have been better, when Sam mistakenly obeyed the words directed at Mary, for the trainer to have praised him for being such a smart and alert fellow?

Training is like building with blocks . . . we shouldn't pile them too high until we are sure the base is solid. If Sam hadn't been pushed so hard at such an early age, he wouldn't have bolted and lost his life.

9. DOG PROBLEMS

DAY-CARE CENTERS . . . FOR DOGS?

There are a lot of people who can't leave their dogs at home all day because their working hours are irregular. Day-care centers, in the large metropolitan areas, have come into existence to fill the dogs' needs. The dogs are picked up each morning and delivered back to the owners each night. They are fed, watered, and walked, and they seem to enjoy the day very much. These centers have become places, in many cases, where untrained dogs spend their days. Many dogs are placed in these centers not because of the irregular working hours of their masters, but because untrained dogs are a problem . . . they howl or tear up the house when left alone.

Even an aggressive dog learns very soon to behave in this group environment. Walk time at the center is exciting for the dogs, and it's amazing that they seem to understand that they have to behave. Any unruly fellow is put in his place. It's interesting that these dogs respond to their daytime trainer very well. In the case of many dogs this is the only real handling they get. Their masters have raised spoiled and pampered "children." These centers are proof that dogs, like children, really want discipline and are happier when they have to be good citizens. The owners of the centers say the unruly dog at home becomes a good fellow at the center, but he doesn't seem to learn from his daytime experience. When he gets back home he's trouble all over again. Since the master at home puts up with it, why should the dog change his ways? He's getting what he wants. That's something any child learns, and fast.

DAY-CARE CENTERS . . .
FOR DOGS?

Some day-care centers pick up the dogs in the morning and deliver them home at the end of the day. It does take care of the problem dog who is a lot of trouble when left alone. It's interesting that even problem dogs seem to give no trouble at the center. They soon learn to be good or they miss out on the fun. *Upper left:* They get ready for the walk to the park. On the street (*right*) they are ladies and gentlemen. They get plenty of exercise playing retrieve, and (*lower right*) the one fellow that starts to act up gets a firm talking to. These dogs do better at the center than at home, which means their handling at home is not good. . . . They're spoiled.

EXERCISE . . . ONE . . . AND TWO . . . AND THREE

138

. . . AND ONE

Some dogs get their own exercise, a do-it-yourself program . . .

EXERCISE . . . ONE . . . AND TWO . . . AND THREE . . . AND ONE

Some day someone is going to invent a treadmill for dogs so they can do all the running they want right at home. Until that happens you're going to have to walk them. That's not the worst thing. Most working people don't get enough exercise anyway, so a brisk walk twice a day will be good for both your dog and your heart.

Many people have the notion that a big dog can't get enough exercise living in a house. It's not so. Dogs can adapt to a way of life just as we can. Country life would be a lot better for all of us, but since it's just not in the cards, we make the best of it . . . and so do our dogs.

There are various ways around the exercise problem. A lot of doormen in big cities earn extra money by walking the dogs in their buildings, and a lot of kids make afterschool money as dog walkers.

When a dog is under good control, there are a number of ways in which he can exercise. A fun way is with a bicycle. A dog that can heel on command will have no trouble running next to a cyclist. There is a lot of exercise in that for all. Another way is a game of simple retrieving. You can give a dog a great amount of exercise by using a stick, a ball, or anything else that takes his fancy. Throwing the object over a fence for him to fetch adds to the fun.

. . . some walk with their masters. Heeling with a bike-riding master means exercise for both of them . . .

. . . Some get away with murder.

THE PROBLEMS

The problems of bad dogs could drive a dog writer to drink. When people discover that a dog writer is in their midst, invariably the subject gets around to curing their dear Fifi's chewing, barking, wetting, snapping . . . the list grows according to the number of cocktail parties one attends. On talking to these people, it becomes evident that they want a gimmick, a magic bone that they can throw to their dogs and next day all will be well, the bad habit gone.

Unfortunately, most people can't tell you what their dog's real problem is. They can only tell you about the objectionable act. Straightening out a problem, once it is set as a pattern, is a very difficult thing to do. It takes animal sense and few people have it. We ask that a dog live by our set of rules. We give human attributes to our dogs, yet we know a dog can't reason. What we don't seem to understand is that difficult as it is for us to deal with an animal that can't reason, it is just as difficult for an animal to deal with a human who can reason. If we want things to change, then the burden is going to have to be on us.

Dogs tend to learn only vices from one another. For example, if you have two dogs living together, and one is a barker and the other is not, they'll both end up as barkers. If you want a dog to be a certain way, 85 percent of what you will get is from your effort and the other 15 percent is from the dog's heredity. These percentage figures may not be scientifically exact, but if you understand your role as trainer this is about what you can expect. Just because you start the dog at the right age doesn't guarantee that no problems will develop. If they do, then you will know where the blame should be put . . . on you as a trainer, not on the dog. You must direct the learning and nip problems in the bud.

Animal sense, that's the big concept for you to work on. Let's take an example and see what those words mean.

Let's say you have a barker. Your neighbors complain to the landlord in your building about this. Of course, hindsight would have prevented the problem in the first place. If barking or any other problem had been a "no, no" when the dog was very young and the problem first cropped up, it could have been corrected more easily. Now that the dog is adult, you may not even know why he's doing it.

To solve this problem you have to figure out why he's a barker. There are two possible reasons: he's self-willed, or he's worried. If he is self-willed, the problem is not too difficult to cure. First, leave the house and stay out until you hear him to start to howl; then return in a huff and give him what for. Make him understand in no uncertain terms that we'll have no more of that. This kind of reasoning a dog *can* understand. He will be able to decide whether the pleasure he gets from the howling is worth the pain of a good licking. You might have to repeat it a few times until he decides.

Recall Chapter 2, where I discussed how to pick a pup. The dominant pup with all the #1's in his score is this same self-willed fellow who was so cute in the litter. Now he's stubborn and headstrong. Even so, you could have shown him as a pup that you were just as strong-willed. It just takes a little more doing with this fellow than it would have taken with the well-adjusted pup who had the #3's in his score. The self-willed pup barks because he wants his way and doesn't want to be left alone. Early correction would have been accomplished by leaving him and returning to catch him in the act. By gradually increasing the time you are out, he'll learn to enjoy a little peace and quiet around the house. With the young pup you won't have to be so severe to get the message through to him.

It's the worrier whose behavior is harder to correct. If you treat the worried dog in the same way as the self-willed one, you are only going to make matters worse. You may cure the howling problem with the worrier by being overbearing, but another problem will crop up.

How do you know if he's a worrier? Some trainers say they can tell by the look in a dog's eyes. This does take experience. In discussing the litter-picking test we showed that the dogs that scored #4's and #5's in the test were the pups inclined toward shyness; they would tend toward being worriers. Of course, worrying can develop after a pup is brought home and is living with you in the big new world. This trait can develop either from the way you handle him or from disturbing things in the environment, or from a combination of both.

What are the signs of a worrier? All animals show certain traits when they're worried. A man waiting outside the hospital delivery room paces up and down. A caged bear walks a figure eight. A worried horse bobs and weaves his head. Children and older persons rock back and forth. A dog runs in circles, or when resting he curls up into a tight ball. If you look you will see a worried look about the eyes of a troubled dog. He'll have a wide-eyed look. He'll continually want to get under furniture. While walking he goes for doorways, as though he wants to get out of the main stream, and most likely he will urinate excessively. You should be able to tell from how he responds to his general training whether he is self-willed or worried. Most people who live with a dog don't take the time to stop and recognize these basic personality traits. Yet they have to be recognized before any progress can be made in correcting the dog's problems.

How does a dog become a worrier? We've already mentioned the stress of the urban environment, noises, movement, and so on. There are a lot of other things in life that disturb a dog. One is the miserable sexual life that most urban dogs have. The pretty bitch in season is saved for one of her own kind, and the dog down the block can get rather uptight about that situation. Even on their outings dogs have no freedom. The walk to the park doesn't give them much of an opportunity to make love. Many an urban dog's whole life is sexless. Sexual frustration has caused serious problems and crimes in our society, yet we tend to ignore that fact when it comes to our dogs. If being a worrier is the only result of sex problems, you're getting off easy; it could result in a noisy or aggressive dog.

There is another innate dog problem. A dog marks a territory that's his possession, but in our crowded streets or parks it becomes a Chinese puzzle that even he couldn't figure out. We go to elaborate lengths and expense to protect our possessions. The dog can't manage this, so it leads to more frustration or worrying. In overcrowded city living, animals, just like men, become suspicious and defensive. Yet the dog who can't mark out his territory in the streets because there are too many dogs in the area is supposed to be a little gentleman when strangers are brought into the house, which he instinctively considers his own domain.

The working dogs have an added problem if their working instinct has not been bred out of them. The terriers, for example, have a rough time if they have no work to do, so they make work. It may not be socially acceptable but a pedestrian's moving legs make good objects to chase, and kids on bicycles are even more fun.

The answer to many of the problems that come up is to give the dog a job that will take his mind off his problems. Take a few minutes each day and make him do his commands. Teach him to fetch, and play the game with him in the park or the livingroom. Let him carry a stick or a rolled-up leash in his mouth when you go for walks. Let a dog have his job and some pride.

Carrying the paper is a good job, or if he's good at heel let him carry his leash. The way to teach this is simple. Open the dog's mouth by applying pressure on each side of his cheeks. When he opens up, slip the paper into his mouth, holding it there and praising him. He'll spit it out until he gets the idea of what you want. Start over. Put the paper in his mouth . . . hold it there and command HOLD. He'll get the idea and learn to love doing it. (*Pictures left to right.*)

Dogs are just like men. They become worriers for two reasons: either they have nothing to do, or too much, and the constant nagging of a boss is a form of overwork. Many dogs start to develop bad habits when they are mature because their masters won't leave them alone. This can take many forms. The nagging trainer worries a dog. He never lets the dog have any peace, always talks to him, and gives him no time off. Guide dogs can become problems if there is constant touch checking by the blind master to "see" what he is up to. It's the same with the dog "lover" who is constantly fondling the dog. Such owners have a hard time understanding why Fido chews on the furniture when they give him so much attention.

Too much stress can be put on a dog by proximity. Man is no different. If two people sit down to talk and one gets too close, the other one will draw back. Did you ever see swallows landing on a telephone wire? They will all be the same distance apart. If one gets too close, the ones next to it will adjust their space.

This is known as the critical distance zone, and all animals, man included, have a certain separation distance at which they feel comfortable. It changes according to circumstances. We city people have learned to put up with a close zone, but it puts stress on us whether we know it or not. Don't nag a dog, let him have his time and place for peaceful privacy, and observe his critical distance zone.

The bored dog grows fat and spends his time sleeping. The pressure of understimulation will eventually cause problems. Many people treat their pets like objects. That doesn't mean they don't love them. The animal has all its basic needs attended to, but there is little overt affection shown. Monotony sets in, and in relieving it something is going to happen. Don't expect the dog to run the dust mop or put things in order while you are out . . . there are more interesting things to do, like howling. If howling is not the answer, maybe getting into the garbage might be fun . . . at least it's creative. Give your dog a game. Train him and keep him active. Teach him some simple tricks. He'll get as much pleasure doing them for you as you will get showing him off, and he'll get pleasure showing off too.

Call all this psychology if you want, but it's better to think of it as animal sense. By no means is this discussion complete . . . that would take a whole book by an animal behaviorist. The important thing for you to understand is that dog problems are not isolated acts. They stem from the lack of early training and/or the stress that you have allowed to develop. If one of the gimmicks cures your dog's bad habit, consider yourself lucky. When you meet me at a cocktail party don't ask me how to cure Fido's problem. You are the one who has all the background information; you have to take the facts, think the complete situation through, and try for your own solution. Then you'll have animal sense, and you'll be as pleased as a pup who has just learned to sit on command.

TOOLS TO HELP SOLVE THE PROBLEMS

The most important tool you will have to use in training a dog is the animal sense that we've been talking about. That combined with the choke collar and leash are the most important tools. Some of the other things that are worth trying are throw cans, tape recorders, and spray cans of vile smelling and ill-tasting substances. These gimmicks can be successful in some cases, so if necessary they should be tried. There is one other item we use for reprimand—the collapsible cage sold for transporting a dog.

You can make the throw cans yourself. Take three or four empty food cans and puncture a hole in the bottom of each. Tie them together with a knotted string through the holes. Then throw this noisemaker when the dog is caught in the act of wrongdoing. I've used it successfully with dogs that chase me on my bicycle.

Some trainers suggest using a tape recorder to give commands and make noise while the master is out. Try it if you have a serious problem, but it's never

A dog has no moral sense. He'll steal and just hope he won't be caught. The cans will scare him and he'll know you don't like it. A dog will learn when he's caught in the act. The noise and clatter will make him remember.

worked for me. The idea that hearing the master's voice will keep the dog in line just doesn't seem to follow. Few if any dogs pay attention to the blare and blast from our radios and television sets. As far as I can figure, it's all background noise to them. In fact, I feel that this method could be detrimental to training. On first hearing your voice the dog may be startled, but he'll soon learn that you are not there and that he doesn't have to pay attention to the sound of your voice since there is no follow-through to your commands.

One of the most effective tools is the Kennel-Aire. This is a folding wire cage used basically for transporting dogs in a station wagon. We always have one set up in the house. The door is left open. Since the dog enjoys a cavelike place to rest, this serves the purpose well. The dog gets a secure feeling in his "room." We use it also as a means of reprimand. Like any naughty child the dog is banished from society by being sent to his "room" and having the door closed. It's worked on children for generations, and it'll work on dogs if they are caught in the act of a wrongdoing and understand why they are being sent off to Siberia.

The best training tool of all is to start with the very young pup and get the job done right from the beginning. Do as the doctors are now doing . . . use preventive medicine . . . then the cures won't be necessary.

BEGGING . . . NOT EVEN A CRUMB

The cute little puppy with the big brown eyes who sits and looks so sad while you eat will turn into a big obnoxious monster who can ruin a pleasant dinner party. Don't let the begging business start. Don't let anyone in the family feed the dog at any time from the table. A dog will never learn to differentiate between when you think it would be permissible and when it would not be acceptable. All he'll learn is that he might get something if he tries.

A dog should have his own bowl and should be fed at a regular time in one specific place. And when you give a dog snacks between meals you are on your way to teaching him to beg. Most trainers use a snack in their training as a reward. I am against this method. For a job well done, praise and a good pat is better than food, and it makes the bond between you and the dog strong. He learns to do the job for you and not his belly. The only exception to this is in teaching the dog to speak.

To stop the friendly puppy when he puts his paws up in your lap to ask for food, firmly put him down on the floor and command "No." If he persists, remove him from the room. With an older dog who wasn't taught his manners as a pup, put the choke collar and leash on him when you start your meal. When he begs, pick up the leash from the floor and give him the corrective jerk and the command NO and send him away. This will tell him that begging is a no, no.

GARBAGE IS TO BE COLLECTED . . . NOT STREWN

There is nothing like returning home to a house that looks like a big garbage pail. Added to that work of man's best friend, the garbage could make the dog sick, which means an added mess to clean up. Also, a chicken bone or two in the garbage could kill the dog. The smells of food are irresistible to a dog. It's almost an impossibility to teach the average dog not to steal food. It is really your responsibility to keep the garbage in a container where the dog can't get at it.

You can try to set up a situation where you catch the dog in the act. This may work, but I doubt that a permanent lesson will be learned unless the choke collar is on. When you catch him in the act of getting into the garbage, a good yank on the collar will scare him and he'll lose his appetite in a hurry.

The only sure way to keep a dog out of the garbage is to teach him from puppyhood to eat only on command. This is done by some trainers to prevent their dogs from being poisoned or eating other harmful things. It's done with the corrective jerk method. When food is placed before the dog he may not take it until he is commanded to do so. If he takes it before the command is given, he gets the jerk with the choke collar instead. He soon learns that to get the food he must wait for the command.

Try spraying the garbage with a special ill-tasting substance that won't hurt the dog; it will teach him to stay away. Some people have tried to cure dogs of getting into the garbage by sprinkling tabasco, mustard, or other hot seasonings on the garbage. It works with some dogs, but just like people, some dogs get to love the stuff.

CHEWING IS FOR FOOD . . . NOT FURNITURE

There is no excuse for destructive chewing, and the habit shouldn't be allowed to develop in the first place. Puppies do go through a period when teething is a discomfort. A few ice cubes in their drinking water will help ease the pain. Better yet, wet a wash cloth and put it in the freezer. Let the pup chew on that . . . it'll relieve the ache.

From the time of puppyhood chewing should be a no, no. Make sure that there are plenty of toys to play with. Rawhide toys are the best, but an old leather glove will do. Rubber balls and such kill dogs. They finally chew off a piece of the soft rubber or plastic toy and swallow it. It gets lodged in their intestines. When the pup starts chewing on something of value, or of *no* value, take it away from him and give him his toy. When he is a pup don't make a big deal of it, but as he gets older, past the teething stage, make sure he understands that you mean business about it.

Sun Dance was a very destructive dog until his master gave him his own toys. The ball is so hard that he can't chew off pieces and swallow them. Rubber toys are dangerous for a dog.

There are repellents on the market that you can spray on things that the dog chews; or alum and water can be mixed and painted on the objects. Often, however, this only leads the dog to chew on other items. After all, you can't spray and paint the whole house.

Leave the choke collar and leash on a dog who seems to persist in chewing the wrong things. Catch him at his handiwork and give him a few good jerks. Let him know what for.

The chewing problem in an adult dog is very serious because there is no way of explaining to him that if he doesn't stop that he'll soon be living in a new home. But it is not all his fault. He's developed this habit out of boredom, fear, or a general feeling of insecurity that you've helped develop in him. If you suspect that he is doing it for a specific reason try to change the situation. Maybe he needs more attention, more exercise, or more companionship. Maybe a cat to keep him company will solve the problem, or you might have to send him off to day care school. This problem does not usually arise in a dog who is well-trained and gets his exercise.

FURNITURE IS FOR PEOPLE

Some people don't mind the dog taking over the furniture. Some don't mind it until they buy new furniture, then they expect the dog to understand that all of a sudden he is dispossessed. Some people allow the dog to sleep with them on their bed, but they can't understand why the dog can't learn to stay off the sofa. Once again, the dog must be made to understand from the beginning. If it's decided that he is to consider the furniture off limits, start him out that way . . . never let him get up on it.

150

What does he do when you leave him alone in the house? Fluff up the cushions and see; he'll leave his mark. If you don't have fluffy cushions, as soon as you return go around and feel the furniture. If he jumped off when he heard the key in the lock, the spot where he was lying will still be warm. If you find body warmth, then you can put the collar on him and give him a few good corrective jerks. A firm "No" at that time will be as good as catching him in the act itself. Some trainers suggest setting mousetraps, hoping they will frighten the dog into staying off the furniture. They place them under newspapers spread out on the cushions. It might work on your dog, but I've never known it to be effective. They seem to learn that after a few strange noises are set off life is as comfortable as ever.

It's better to make a real comfortable place for the dog, a place away from drafts. Give him a good pad and a view from a corner . . . he'll feel secure there. And, oh yes, you stay out of his bed.

BARKING . . . A WAY TO BREAK THE LEASE

I have already said some things about the excessive barker. I've suggested that you leave the house and wait outside for him to start his racket and then stomp in and enforce the reprimand. By leaving the collar and leash on him you can make the corrective jerk quickly when you storm back into the house. Possibly the leash being dragged around all day will remind him that you might show up and give him what for. All this might work, but a better system is a more positive approach. If you are out all day, arrange for a dog sitter to take him out when you leave. On the first day have the dog walker return the dog when you return. On the second day have him arrive five minutes before you get there. Each day have the time the dog is alone in the house increased some more. We're counting on the exercise and breaking the dog's routine to help him forget his bad habit.

JUMPING ON PEOPLE . . . A PROBLEM OF AFFECTION

An enthusiastic dog shows his love by jumping up. It's his way of greeting you. You greet your friends, some with a kiss, and the dog wants to do the same thing. I personally don't object to the dog's greeting me by jumping up . . . so it costs me a few dollars a year for dry cleaning. It's unfair to guests and friends, however, to allow your dog to greet them. The easiest way to train a dog not to jump up is to never allow him to do it with you or your friends.

If he does jump up while walking on leash the corrective jerk will soon train him not to. When it happens off lead the dog should be put down. The method to use will depend on the size of the dog. With a big dog, bringing the knee up and pushing him backward will accomplish the trick. Since he was expecting a friendly

Of course a dog should be friendly but not to the point of jumping up to show his pleasure. A small dog can be pushed down with your hand. A big dog requires stronger measures. The knee in the chest won't really hurt him . . . it comes as a surprise. It'll only take a few knees in the chest to stop this.

response, he'll be so astonished that he won't try it again. With smaller dogs, the hand can be used. With the flat of the palm, push him back and down. Command "No" while doing it. After the correction is made, praise him, because he's really trying to be nice.

THE SENSUOUS DOG . . . LOVERS ALL

We've spoken about the unfortunate sex life of most dogs. The female usually comes into heat twice a year, but the male can be sexually aroused at any time. For him to mount a child or an adult's leg is very embarrassing and must be considered a no, no . . . to put it mildly. The correction is made with the corrective jerk using the collar and leash. I'm sure the sex drive varies from dog to dog. A highly sexed dog that is segregated from females is a real problem. Mating won't necessarily stop his drive, but plenty of exercise can help a lot.

Another bad habit males have is to sniff under women's skirts. This can be corrected by firmly using the jerk method. Give the collar a sharp yank and command "No."

CARS . . . PROBLEMS FOR THE DOGS TOO

When man and dog became friends those many eons ago, they both got around by running on their feet. The dog didn't seem to mind any of the inventions man brought along except for one, the car. With the right handling dogs get to love car travel, but for many it means problems. If a dog vote could be taken, I'm sure he'd be for banning the automobile.

To get even for this invention many dogs chase cars, seemingly to drive them off the road. I've seen all sorts of tricks tried to stop this dangerous habit. With the help of an assistant in the back seat, a bucket of water thrown on the dog may deter him. The same procedure with ammonia water in a water pistol has cured some dogs. One trick that I saw cure a dog was to have the car stop and the assistant turn out to be the dog's master. The dog was given a good thrashing. He never tried it again.

Perhaps dogs chase cars because of their hunting instinct, but knowing that fact doesn't help cure the problem. Many dogs have been killed by cars, and years ago one of my best friends was killed in a car avoiding a dog that ran out into the road to chase him. If you can't cure this habit, you should keep your dog confined at all times.

Car sickness is another common problem with dogs. Most trainers feel sure that the source can be traced back to a bad early experience with a car. A dog should become acclimated to a car before he is taken for his first ride. Let him play in and around it for a time before the motor is started up. Don't feed or give a pup water before he is taken on his first jaunt. If he seems unduly nervous after the first ride, let him spend more time in the car so he gets used to the smells and makes it part of his territory. You can even feed him a few times in the car. When you are about to take him for the next ride, be sure you use a fun voice and make it seem that you are enjoying it too. Of course, if you start from the very beginning with him, all this will not be necessary . . . car sickness usually appears in dogs who get their first ride at about five months of age.

You should check carefully on a pup who suddenly develops car sickness. He's had some traumatic experience. People don't seem to realize how hot a car gets in midsummer, even with the windows partially open. I once opened a car at a shopping center to save a dog's life. The inside was like an oven, and in panic the dog was hurling himself against the windows. I'm sure that such a dog would never want to ride in a car again. Heat prostration is a very frightening thing to experience. The cause of sickness may also be fumes, backfiring, or the motion of the car itself. Keep an eye on a pup when he travels with you. Take it easy until he gets to like to travel or you can have many an outing ruined.

As for the dog that loves to travel in the car, make him learn SIT-STAY under control. Use the jerk method to keep him in his place. Never allow him to bark at dogs outside, and remind him from time to time that he's a passenger and not the driver. There is no need for him to hang his head out the window. It's very bad for his eyes.

10. THE ALARM DOG

A NEW KIND OF PROTECTION DOG

The headline in *The New York Times* read: "Boy, 6, Fatally Attacked by Guard Dogs." The subhead on the story stated, "Two Shepherds Apparently Escaped From the Area They Patrolled." Every so often stories of this nature appear in the news. It's an interesting fact that the same breed of dog that can be trained as a man-stopper and killer if need be is also trained to be a guide dog for the blind. The same day that the headline was in the paper, I happened to see a guide dog leading a blind person in a very heavy traffic situation. The dog started to make a serious mistake, but a couple of people stepped in and brought the blind person and dog back safely to the curb. It was an error on the dog's part, but it was quickly straightened out. An error on the part of a dog trained as an attack dog is a deadly business that's hard to stop.

Attack dogs are trained in a step-by-step system of agitating the dog and at the same time building his confidence. They are trained so as to be agitated to the point where they can kill if necessary. They can be put on the alert with an almost inaudible command and sent into action with one word. They can be stopped in the middle of a bite. Their training is magnificent, but there are only a few trainers who can do a perfect job with these dogs and make them 100 percent reliable. There is really no place for these dogs in the hands of the public. A do-it-yourself course in guard dog training would be like encouraging the public to play Russian roulette.

ALARM DOG

We would like to introduce a concept in training that we'll call an alarm dog. We have already seen that many dog owners deliberately pick the large breeds. They make no bones about their choice. The added inconvenience of a big dog even in a small house is compensated for by the feeling of protection and security the big brute gives. One man who was walking his dog in the town park told me, "I walk around the streets and jog every morning through the park with my Doberman running by my side. I'm sick and tired of being harassed by a bunch of punks. I hope the word gets around that I've got the meanest dog on the block." He started to laugh as he continued, "Actually, I think she'd run if anyone tried to mug me, but neither my wife nor I have been bothered since we got the dog. She is well-mannered, and I'd go any place with her. After all, who is to know whether or not she has been trained as an attack dog? She looks tough and her bark sounds as though she means business. I just think a mugger would decide not to take a chance."

The mere presence of this dog is like giving an alarm. The man went on to tell me that he had gone to a lot of trouble to train his Doberman to be faultless on the street. The dog heeled with precision. He figured that even a potential mugger would know that an ill-trained dog, one that showed bad manners, pulled on the leash, jumped up, or didn't pay attention to the handler, would not have been trained for attack work. All working dogs, whether they are attack dogs, Seeing-Eye dogs, or just well-trained pets, carry themselves with dignity and have a businesslike air about them.

What we've said so far is that certain breeds of dogs, by their very presence, can alarm strangers—but any dog, no matter what size, can be trained to be an alarm dog. The alarm dog will be a safe dog to have in any kind of family situation. The alarm dog will take no protective action. His job will be to deter trouble, not to solve it. For example, all burglars would agree that if they had prior information on the places they were going to knock off, they'd steer clear of houses that had dogs. A barking dog could be an added danger for them.

There are specific jobs you can give your dog to make him truly an alarm dog, and they are not hard to teach. One job is to announce anyone who is approaching your place. The way to train the dog to announce is first to train him to bark on command. We showed you this with the German shepherd pup, Sam, pages 107 to 111. Once the dog learns to bark on command, it is just a matter of giving him the idea of when you want him to bark on his own initiative. If each time your doorbell rings or there is a knock at the door, you command the dog to bark, he'll very soon get the drift of what you want. Praise him and make a fuss over him when he does as commanded. Soon you will see that the transfer is made, and you won't have to give the vocal command. There are a few refinements you can add. Have *everyone* announced. The plan here calls for two friends to come calling on you. The second friend should arrive a few minutes after the first one. The dog should learn to "greet" all parties and not to assume that they are together just because the first guest is still with the master. You should give the dog the command to bark if he fails to do so when the second person arrives. Do this over and over until he gets the message.

You should decide whether you want your alarm dog to announce the person

before he actually rings or knocks. Experiments show that a dog hears about seven times better than a man. There are a few ways to take advantage of this great hearing ability. If you want your dog to bark on first hearing the approaching footsteps, command him to do so as soon as you hear the person coming . . . he'll get the idea; then he'll do it before you hear anything.

The dog's sense of smell is as good as his hearing. A friend of ours used her dog's senses, both sound and smell, to make her life alone in an apartment a little safer. One day, before she got her dog, she was greeted by a burglar upon returning to her apartment. Fortunately, he was just as scared on being discovered as she was on discovering him. He ran without harming her. That little experience convinced her to get a dog. She chose a black Labrador.

Our friend trained her Lab by the bark-on-command method and added her own innovation to the alarm system. She taught him to enter the apartment and scout it out first. Taking a chapter from the training of the plant security dog, she applied it to her alarm dog. Here is the way she went about it, with the help of a few friends.

When her dog was about six months old, well along in his general training and already barking on command, she had some friends play the part of intruders. A friend should hide in a closet or alcove. As the handler enters the apartment with the dog on lead, he should give the command SEARCH. While the handler is walking the dog through the apartment on a leash, the "intruder" should make a noise such as the scraping of a shoe on the floor. When the dog hears the noise and gets the scent too, he'll respond. If it's a bark, praise him. If it's a startled response, like ears and head up, the handler should give the "secret" command to bark. It'll be a game for the dog and your friends. The "intruder" should hide at different places and make different kinds of noises to attract the dog. As the dog gets the idea that he is to find the person and bark, then the whole thing should be done with the "intruder" being very quiet. This is to teach the dog to use his nose as well as his ears. If the dog does not make the discovery by scent alone, the intruder should burst upon the dog, make a loud noise to frighten him, and then flee from the apartment. This is to startle the dog. The next time he'll announce the intruder before the intruder startles him.

The more friends you can get to act as intruders the easier this training is going to be, because the dog quickly gets to know the smell of one "intruder." After a few weeks of it, and when you think the dog has gotten the idea, do it with the dog off leash. The idea is to get him to carry out the whole search while you stand in the hall, so he can warn you before you are trapped inside your own apartment.

Remember Sam? Mary started him out to be an alarm dog. The first step in the training was to have him bark on their secret command . . . when she cleared her throat. To Sam it was fun. Turn the page to see the next step.

THE STREET ALARM

Very rarely, if ever, do we read in the news about anyone being mugged while walking his dog. It's a comfort to have a big dog on a leash when you spot some unsavory characters walking toward you on a lonely street. This is the situation where it's very handy to have the dog trained to bark on command as you walk with him. Nobody will bother you then. Of course, a big dog is going to sing out with more authority, but many people are now training little dogs to bark on command, as alarm dogs. The theory is that it's the noise itself that will deter the mugger. As one woman put it, "I keep my eyes open when I'm walking on the streets in the evening, and if I see a situation that I don't like, I command Fritz to bark. Many of the people that I was afraid were going to give me trouble crossed the street to get out of my way. A barking dog seems to do the trick, and we've never been bothered."

As we saw earlier with Sam, Mary's secret command to bark was the clearing of the throat. You can keep the dog trained to bark on command on your walks without needing any assistance or special set-ups. If the dog does not sustain his barking long enough, repeat the "silent" command and have him start again. He should learn that he is to continue until you give him a signal to stop. You can give him a pat, command "OK, good fellow," and go on about your business. Keep testing him, and each time a questionable character walks your way, especially if the street is deserted, start your alarm going.

We saw how Mary taught Sam to bark on command and she made it a game. But then Sam was killed by a car and she started another dog. His name is Damnit. He was handled the same way as Sam and he, too, barked on the secret command when Mary cleared her throat. The next step in the training of the alarm dog is to change the barking from fun to serious sounding business. The series of pictures that follow on the next five pages show how this is accomplished. An assistant, unknown to the dog, is needed and his training tool is an ordinary house mop. Mary and Damnit came walking down the street. They were accosted by the mop-wielding assistant.

1 . . . The assistant starts the attack. He shouts and jumps around, making a commotion. He does not strike the dog but waves the mop in front of his nose. Damnit pulls back not knowing what this is all about. Mary gives her command by clearing her throat but Damnit doesn't respond . . .

2 . . . the attacker advances and Damnit is obviously confused. The barking command is repeated. The attack is continued . . .

3 . . . The dog retreats and the attacker advances shaking the mop. Damnit has now backed off as far as he can get. Mary continues her command to bark.

4 . . . When the attacker has Damnit backed off as far as he can go, he himself backs away. This is the important part. The dog now will recover and go on the offensive. As the attacker and mop back off, the dog, with renewed confidence, will start forward. The command to bark now registers . . .

160

5 . . . the mop is pulled back and the dog now wants to get to that thing. He strains on the leash, and that is what we want him to do. Mary is encouraging him with praise and the clearing of the throat command.

6 . . . Now the mop and the attacker have retreated and Mary holds Damnit back with the leash but pushes him ahead with her leg. While she gives the bark command she wants him to strain forward.

7 . . . The attack starts again. This time Damnit is not frightened. He's ready! Mary gives the command to bark and . . .

8 . . . Damnit charges forward and Mary lets him go to the end of the leash. He learned that the command means to be nasty and that the frightening thing, the attacking mop, will retreat. With Mary's praise, he learns that that is what she wants. Now, on the next page, you see what Damnit can do on the street . . . on command!

162

11. HEALTH, WELFARE, AND TIPS

THE DOG'S BODY LANGUAGE

Training, like communication, is a two-way street. A smart trainer will learn to understand the dog's language. The dog gives some audible signals the trainer must interpret. Different tones of barks convey the dog's mood. Even a novice knows that the bark of greeting differs from the fearful or warning bark. And the dog's body language will tell how serious his growl or bark is. In town, where you are constantly meeting strange dogs, it can pay off to know the signs the dog uses to communicate his mood.

A dog that wants to be submissive and friendly will avoid eye-to-eye contact. His ears will be flattened against his head; his tail will be low and will wag slowly. Some dogs will roll over on their back to show their submission, or they may crawl toward you on their belly. Unfortunately, some will piddle, which is an act acceptable in the dog world; others will lift a forepaw as if to shake hands. Many dogs will give a greeting grin much like a human smile. This is often misread as aggression by those who do not know the signs. When the dog grins and shows his teeth to a person, his head is pointed upward or turned to the side and his eyes do not make contact with that person.

A dog has another signal for play; it's the bow. His front paws are extended so that his hindquarters are higher than his shoulders. His tail is held high and wags, his head is erect, and his ears are forward. He may prance about and show he wants to play; his growl and bark are fun sounds.

The body language of the threat is the one we should all be familiar with. Threats come in many degrees, from snapping at the air to an attack and biting. The signal of trouble is the direct stare and the snarl. A high head with ears forward means that the dog is in no way submissive. The lips are pulled back to bare the teeth for action, and the hackles on the rump and neck are raised to give

If you met this dog, you might be scared with all the teeth showing. He's grinning at his master . . . it's his way of saying hello, but half the people he meets are frightened to go near him . . . the poor thing is misunderstood.

him a bigger look. He comes to full height and seems to stand on his toes. Don't be fooled by a wagging tail. It will be a slow wag in an aggressive dog, and often on the actual attack the tail is lifted over his back to get it out of the way.

Often a dog is not sure of his own mood and shows it. While he's putting on an aggressive act his head and tail will give him away. If the head and tail bob up and down, it means he's not sure whether he wants to be aggressive or submissive. One step toward an agitated dog will show his real meaning. If he doesn't back down and gets even more excited, watch out. If he momentarily drops his tail and moves his weight to his hindquarters, he's probably bluffing.

If a dog is a fear biter, his ears will be flat against his head, hackles up, and weight shifted back. His tail will gradually be lowered and tucked between his legs. He makes all the sounds of the aggressive dog, but he usually won't attack unless you move in on him.

DOG
OVERPOPULATION

Spayed Females. Today there is a very serious dog population problem in both our urban and suburban areas. One major Eastern city picked up 17,000 stray dogs last year. That was an increase of 300 over the year before. Sixty-one thousand dogs in that city were turned in to the SPCA as unwanted, of which 55,000 had to be destroyed. Another organization in that city disposed of an additional 12,000 dogs. Man's best friend isn't making out too well. Hundreds of unwanted dogs each year are taken by their owners to wooded areas outside the cities and turned loose. Many areas have dangerous dog packs roaming and hunting for their own survival.

It is estimated that the dog population in the United States has doubled in the past five years, and many of the 60 million dogs, with their owners, are gravitating to the cities and surrounding communities. Some of the shelters that try to find new homes for dogs have a plan for controlling the dog population. They charge a nominal fee for the dog and a $25 deposit, which the new owner will get back if he has the dog neutered. The operation usually costs from $35 to $100, but many vets are cooperating with the shelters and doing the job, for families that can't afford it, by accepting the $25 return deposits.

Females that have been spayed make fine pets. Their personalities are not altered and it is an old wives' tale that the operation makes them fat and lazy. As in people, dogs become overweight by eating too much; this is discussed on pages 168–169. Many dog lovers believe a bitch should be allowed to become a mother once, to fulfill herself. As liberated women will tell you, this is not necessary for females of any kind. Some parents breed their pet as an educational experience for their children, but in the city this brings on so many unexpected problems and so much expense that they seldom do it again. The breeding of dogs, especially in our cities, should be left to the professionals.

For a time, drugs were used to postpone heat in the female, but vets advice against this method of birth control because it has produced too many adverse side effects in the bitch. New inoculation techniques are being tried, but at the moment they are not perfected. The best solution is spaying.

Many a family has gotten all excited when they thought pups were on the way, only to discover their female was having a false pregnancy. It happens to some dogs about nine weeks after the normal heat; they show signs of enlarged abdomen, have swelling around the nipples, and may even produce milk. Your vet may give hormone injections in exaggerated cases, but the condition will run its course without treatment in three to five weeks.

DIET

Diet is especially important for a young, rapidly growing pup. Don't feed him only the food he prefers; get him used to eating what is good for him. If he refuses, let him go hungry . . . he'll change his mind and learn to eat what's put in front of him. An all-meat diet will not supply the nutrients needed, in spite of what the television commercials say. Feeding a dog leftover scraps from your table is not a very good idea. They will not form a balanced diet, and the amounts will vary. A well-balanced diet consists of protein, carbohydrates, vitamins, minerals, and fats . . . dogs can do without starch.

There are three basic kinds of dog foods available: dry foods, sometimes referred to as cereals, containing about 8 percent water; semimoist foods, individually packaged servings that look like ground meat, containing 25 percent water; and canned foods, which are about 75 percent water. Canned foods do not give a complete balanced diet and are expensive. The commercial dry cereals are the best buy for the money and do provide a well-balanced diet. The semidry foods do also; just add water and serve.

The commercial cereals and semidry foods are so good that supplementary foods are not necessary. Many people like to add a small amount of meat to make the meal more attractive for the dog and a teaspoon of corn oil in a pup's food to give his coat a luster. The adult dog would get a tablespoon of the oil mixed into his food for his coat.

At one time it was considered good practice to load a pup with extra calcium. But with the new commercial dry and semidry foods, these added supplements are a waste of money and in some cases are not good for the dog. Let your vet advise you about supplements . . . very few dogs need them.

Dry cereals can be bought in the supermarkets in bags of up to fifty pounds. In some areas the largest bags can be bought only from feed stores. The semidry foods are relatively new. They come packaged in small servings. Some are marketed in a three-ounce size and others come six ounces to the serving. Most grocery stores carry the canned food.

If you insist on playing chef for your dog, a balanced diet can be produced by combinations of meat (beef, horsemeat, lamb, kidney, liver, poultry), cooked fish, milk, cooked eggs (dogs can't digest the white of a raw egg), cottage cheese, cereals, cooked vegetables, and cooked fruit.

Bones are not essential in a dog's diet. Hard dog biscuits do a far better job of keeping teeth clean, and it's better to have a few crumbs on the rug than grease all over the house. If you do give the dog bones, give him only heavy beef bones. Shin bones are the best. Pork, veal, lamb, fish, and chicken bones easily splinter and can cause severe intestinal problems or even kill the dog.

Water is an essential part of the diet and should always be available, except for very young puppies. They'll swim in it and make a mess, or they'll drink too much and not be hungry for their meals.

The *number of meals* a dog gets a day will vary with his age. A young pup of seven weeks gets three meals a day; at six months it's two meals unless he cuts one out himself. A dog of one year of age or older gets one meal a day.

The *time to feed* depends on when you want the dog to sleep. If he's to be a watchdog, he should be alert at night, so feed him in the morning and let him sleep all day. Keep the feeding the same time each day . . . but the dog won't let you forget. His stomach becomes an excellent alarm clock.

The *quantity of food* varies with each dog. Good judgment and a little experimentation are going to be necessary. The feeding chart below is a beginning point; it's for your guidance only. All dogs, whether miniature or monster, can be fed the same diet—the only difference is the amount. You are going to have to watch and see how your dog does and make changes accordingly.

For a long time it was thought that pups should be like butterballs. This is wrong. It is becoming very evident that a pup that carries too much weight for his bone structure could be headed for hip displasia, a serious disease that cripples far too many dogs. Although this disease of the rear hip joints may be hereditary, experiments have shown that overweight pups have a tendency to develop it.

Nutrition is just as important for your dog as it is for your child. Good nutrition can even cure bad behavioral problems. Today there are products on the market that are completely balanced diets—table scraps are not even necessary. One of the problems we people have is that we think the dog should be eating our food, so many manufacturers use dyes to make the dog food appealing to the housewife. The dog couldn't care less. I personally use the Iams dry food products, which are easy to handle and like all the better-quality varieties give me a consistent, fixed-formula, balanced diet. Most of the dog foods sold in supermarkets and on TV do not have fixed formulas and they change according to the market price of the ingredients—you pay for what you get. Inconsistency in foods produces a stress in a dog that can have many undesirable results, such as diarrhea, besides behavioral ones. The better the nutrition the better the dog can resist parasites and other diseases. The sugar content in most semimoist foods is too high, and we have come to learn that a sugar "high" can make kids or dogs go bananas. With canned foods we are buying 74 to 76 percent water. Protein is very important in a dog's diet. Most manufacturers use soybean because it is cheap, but although it is a good source of protein for man, the dog's short intestinal tract makes it a very inefficient food for the dog. Yet manufacturers using it can claim a higher quantity of protein, although that does not mean high quality (usable) for the dog. Also, don't cut your dog's food down in the summer as we humans do. On the hottest summer day a dog will use the same amount of calories as on the coldest day in winter.

FEEDING CHART
BY EDWARD GRANO, JR., D. V. M.

			AMOUNT PER FEEDING		
AGE No. Feedings Per Day	SIZE	Weight in lbs.	DRY 1 cup = 8 oz. by volume	SOFT-MOIST° 1 burger = ½ pkg.	CANNED 1 can = 14½ oz.– 15½ oz.
Weaning to 3 Months 3 Times Daily or Self-Feeding	Small Breeds Medium Breeds Large Breeds Very Large Breeds	3–6 6–12 12–20 15–25	⅓–½ cup ½–¾ cup ¾–1⅓ cups 1–1½ cups	⅕–⅓ pkg. ⅓–½ pkg. ⅔–1 pkg. ¾–1 pkg.	3½–5½ oz. 6¼–9½ oz. 10–14 oz. 11¾–16½ oz.
3–5 Months 3 Times Daily or Self-Feeding	Very Small Breeds Small Breeds Medium Breeds Large Breeds Very Large Breeds	3–10 5–15 12–25 15–35 25–50	½–1 cup ⅔–1⅓ cups 1⅛–2 cups 1½–2⅔ cups 2–3⅓ cups	⅓–⅔ pkg. ½–1 pkg. ¾–1⅓ pkg. 1–1¾ pkg. 1⅓–2⅓ pkg.	4⅔–11 oz. 7⅓–15⅓ oz. 13⅓–22 oz. 15⅔–29⅔ oz. 22⅔–38 oz.
5–7 Months 2 Times Daily or Self-Feeding	Very Small Breeds Small Breeds Medium Breeds Large Breeds Very Large Breeds	4–12 12–24 20–35 35–50 50–90	¾–1⅔ cups 1⅔–2¾ cups 2½–4 cups 4–5 cups 5–6 cups	½–1 pkg. 1¼–1¾ pkg. 1¾–2¾ pkg. 2¾–3½ pkg. 3½–5⅓ pkg.	8–18½ oz. 20–31 oz. 29–44 oz. 45–57 oz. 57–83 oz.
7–10 Months 2 Times Daily or Self-Feeding	Very Small Breeds Small Breeds Medium Breeds Large Breeds Very Large Breeds	5–15 12–25 25–45 45–70 70–100	1–2 cups 2⅛–3⅓ cups 3½–4½ cups 4⅔–6¼ cups 6¼–8½ cups	⅔–1½ pkg. 1½–2½ pkg. 2½–3 pkg. 3⅓–4 pkg. 4–6 pkg.	10½–23 oz. 23½–37 oz. 40–51 oz. 52–69 oz. 70–94 oz.
Adult 1 Time Daily or Self-Feeding	Very Small Breeds Small Breeds Medium Breeds Large Breeds Very Large Breeds	6–12 12–25 25–50 50–90 90–175	1–2 cups 2–3½ cups 3½–6 cups 6½–9½ cups 9½–13½ cups	¾–1½ pkg. 1–2⅓ pkg. 2–3½ pkg. 3½–5⅓ pkg. 5⅓–9½ pkg.	12–23 oz. 23–37 oz. 37–57 oz. 57–85 oz. 86–152 oz.

° One package Prime or Top Choice equals 6 oz. One Gaines-burger equals 3 oz. (½ package).

With the dry foods in a gravity feeder it's possible to allow the dog to feed himself, but feeding is so important and so closely associated with the training that it's good for the trainer to feed the dog.

The problem eater is usually the overfed dog. Twenty minutes after the dog's meal is put down any food he hasn't eaten should be taken up. Let him learn that it's eat now or never. If you take your dog on a trip, it may be hard for him to eat under strange circumstances. Let him get settled down before food is offered to him. After a hard run, dogs should be given plenty of time to cool off and rest before their main meal is given to them.

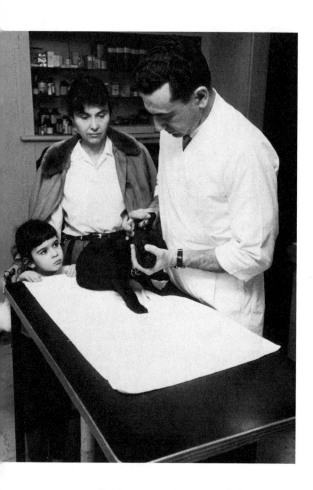

THE VET

You've got to have confidence in your vet, just as your dog has confidence in you. Don't choose him for his office furniture. Instead, make these observations. How does the place smell? Is it immaculate? Does he handle the dog with a sure touch? Is he interested? Is he a warm guy? Does he communicate? Does he seem professional? Does he seem to want to run a beauty parlor instead of an animal hospital? Are his hands clean? Is his lab coat clean? What about his fees?

Find out all you can about the vets in your area. Ask your neighbors, then make up your own mind. Once you've picked your vet, stick with him. A vet who knows you and your dog is more valuable to both of you than a stranger who does not have the dog's history.

You're the one who's going to have to communicate with the vet for your dog. You'll have to recognize symptoms and observe unusual conditions. We don't want to make a veterinarian out of you; you should not try to assume his responsibilities. Your job is to give your vet information so he can solve your dog's medical problems and then to follow his instructions with your pet.

170

DOG PARASITES

Scratching bothers a dog just as much as it does a person. A clean dog, free of *parasites,* won't scratch any more than you will, but a dog with fleas isn't going to stop until you do something about his nonpaying guests. Summer is the worst time of year for parasites. Fleas, lice, ticks and mosquitoes are a real problem for the dog and the owner. Fleas can carry tapeworm and typhus; ticks can carry Rocky Mountain spotted fever and typhus; and mosquitoes can carry heartworm. The most common problem is the itching irritation they cause the dog and all too often you, the owner.

Careful grooming is the first step in the control of all the external parasites. Look under the legs, in the ears, and between the pads on the feet. A parasite that often gets on the dog when he walks in the grass is the tick. Once it gets on the dog's feet it won't move up his leg very fast, so a check on the paws and between the pads after a walk will catch many a tick before it can start causing trouble. On most dogs you should be able to feel the lump caused by the tick; examination consists of ruffling the hair against the way it grows so that you'll be able to see the skin.

The control of fleas and ticks is no joke if your house becomes infested. One female tick can lay as many as two to three thousand eggs, and they can live two months without food. You can see that if only 25 percent survive you'll have a real problem. Both ticks and fleas, especially the latter, like humans as well as dogs. There are a number of good products on the market for the dog and your house. It's important to rid not only the dog of the parasites but his quarters and your house as well. Otherwise, in a few weeks they'll reinfest the animal, and the cycle will start all over. Spray cans are the easiest to use; powders can be messy. There are quiet aerosol cans that will not frighten the dog.

Professional care is needed if *mange* is suspected. It is positively identified by microscopic examination. There are two kinds; the most difficult to cure looks like moth-eaten patches that start on the head and face. It is caused by mites burrowing inside the hair follicles and is called follicular or Demodectic mange. In the other kind, Sarcoptic mange, the mites burrow into the skin, producing an inflammation that appears redder and more raised than in demodex. Itching is intense. A more common name is scabies, and it can be transferred to humans.

Ear mites live in the ear canal, produce itching and a brownish-black discharge. They can be passed to other dogs. It's best to get professional help for these mites since the ear is such a sensitive area. Your vet can treat them with an insecticide.

Ringworm isn't a worm at all; it's a fungus infection of the skin, contagious to humans. It causes an oval, raised lesion that starts about the size of a nickel and gets progressively bigger. Professional treatment is required. The fungus first attacks the hair itself, which becomes dry and brittle. The vet will clip and remove the hair in and around the area and treat the skin, which also becomes infected and dry, with iodine or a fungicide.

Worms are one of the more serious and least understood puppy problems. Some people feel that dogs should be wormed routinely, but this is wrong. However, there should be a routine monthly microscopic examination of the stool until a dog is six months old and twice a year after that. Worms lower a dog's resistance and make other illnesses more serious, so it is best not to wait for symptoms to show.

Symptoms differ according to the kind of worm that has taken up residence in your pet: roundworm, tapeworm, whipworm, or hookworm. He may scratch; his coat will be dry and his skin scaly. A tapeworm infection will cause a ravenous appetite in some dogs, whereas in other cases the dog will lose his appetite and deteriorate to a poor condition. His eyes will appear dull and he'll act listless. Diarrhea usually accompanies hookworm and whipworm. With tapeworm he may drag his rear end on the ground, but this could also indicate that the anal glands need to be emptied.

Worm medicines are not entirely safe for your dog, and it could be that other problems are present to complicate matters, so let your vet make the decisions.

Another worm that was at one time confined to the Southern United States, where the mosquito was so prevalent, is the heartworm. Unfortunately, it has now become a problem in all parts of North America. The mosquito passes an immature form of the worm from dog to dog. The adult worm lives in the heart and adjacent large blood vessels. It damages the heart, lungs, liver, and kidneys and causes the dog to have difficulty breathing, to cough, to tire easily, to become listless, and to lose weight. When the disease reaches this stage it can be cured, except that a lot of damage has already been done. If not treated in the advanced stages it will cause death. The only way to detect heartworm in the early stages is through a simple blood test. If found early, it can be cured before it does any damage. There is no vaccine to protect against heartworm, but there are two methods of preventing infection. One is a daily medication that should be given all through the mosquito season and continued for two months after the season has passed. It can be given year-round in warm climates. The other is an injection twice a year to kill any worms that have started to develop. Heartworm is a serious business, and your vet will know if it is prevalent in your area.

OTHER DOG AILMENTS

Eczema, or moist dermatitis (sometimes called hot spot), is not a fully understood skin disease, and it may or may not be caused by one of the parasites. Many vets feel it is caused by fleas or by an allergy. Warm weather also seems to be a factor, as red and yellow patches appear, angry-looking and wet. Too many baths can also bring on eczema. In persistent cases the vet should do the treating.

Distemper is the major dog killer. It is a virus disease for which there is no cure as yet. If your pup should get it, his chances of survival are slim, and it is best to follow your vet's advice whether to try treatment or put the puppy to sleep. I have tried to buck the inevitable and nurse a stricken pup; it was torment for the family and cruel to the dog.

Early symptoms are loss of appetite, high fever, diarrhea, nausea, a discharge at the eyes and nose, a dry cough, and a sensitivity to light. Sometimes the first sign is a spasmodic chewing as if the dog had something caught in his mouth. Distemper spreads with terrible ease. The virus is transmitted through the urine, feces, nasal discharge, and saliva. It can even be transmitted through the air and carried by the owners of sick dogs.

Although distemper cannot be cured, it is possible to prevent it. For starters, it's very helpful, but not absolutely necessary, to know some things about the pup's mother. And, of course, your vet must know the complete medical history of the pup itself, specifically the kind of shots the pup has had and the dates on which they were given.

Here is how you protect the dog from this biggest killer. Almost every bitch passes on to her pups a natural immunity against diseases, including distemper. All pups in the litter get the same amount of protection, but the amount will differ from litter to litter from the same bitch. However, unless the bitch is tested just before she whelps you will not know how long the immunity she passes on will last in the pups. Few bitches pass on no immunity; some pass on enough to last the pups until they are sixteen weeks old. The average is about eight or nine weeks. This length of time is the unknown factor. If the pup is given a protective shot while his mother's immunity is still in his system, the protective shot will not take, and the dog will have no protection.

Here is the procedure. For pups under nine weeks, in a clean environment with no contact with other dogs, no shots are given. If the dog comes from a kennel or a pet shop and his history is not known, do not take the chance that the mother's immunity will protect him. For such a dog, under nine weeks old, a temporary live virus distemper or measle vaccine is given. If the mother's protection is in the system the shot won't take, but if the pup is unprotected at this age the vaccination will take effect. This puppy shot can be given at the age of six weeks and repeated again at the eighth week. At nine weeks of age all pups should get an adult dose of live virus vaccine. To guarantee that it took and that the mother's protection did not interfere with the immunization, the shot should be repeated four or five weeks later. Now, at the age of thirteen or fourteen weeks, 95 percent of all dogs will be protected. To be extra safe, and to make sure your pup is not part of the 5 percent that are not protected, he should receive another shot between the sixteenth and seventeenth weeks. From then on the shot should be repeated once a year.

You can now see why, in a city, it's important to keep the dog isolated when you bring him home at seven weeks of age. A nine-week-old pup, with his first two protective shots, is safe to take out. Some people like to wait a little longer . . . it's a good idea to wait as long as convenient to make sure the immunization is well established in the pup's system. It's important in this procedure that the vet use live virus vaccine and not kill-tissue vaccine.

Hepatitis is similar to distemper, and a protective vaccine is usually given in combination with the distemper shot. In addition to distemper symptoms, the puppy's tummy hurts, and he'll often hump himself up to relieve the pain. The inside of the mouth becomes fiery red or yellowish, indicating a generalized infection. The disease strikes rapidly and spreads.

Leptospirosis is a disease that attacks the kidney and liver. It is contracted from the droppings or urine of infected rats or dogs. If you live in a rat-infested area, a protective shot should be given every six months. Also dry food should be kept in a closed metal container. Discard any sacks or containers that rats have broken into. Droppings or infected urine might be present, and when your dog eats the food he'll get infected. Symptoms include: deep yellow urine with a strong smell; vomiting of bile, frothy white or yellow; stiff muscles, especially in the hindquarters; widespread hemorrhaging, diarrhea, eye and nasal discharge, and jaundice. It is possible for humans with an open skin wound to catch the disease by contact with an infected dog.

Rabies a few decades ago was a common and feared disease among dogs. Although it has been largely controlled in this country, it is far too deadly to be complacent about. It is transmitted only by a bite, by which infected saliva is injected into the tissues of another animal. It is important that you never try to handle a dog that you suspect of having rabies.

Symptoms of rabies begin with a marked change in behavior—a friendly dog will avoid people, or a shy one will become overfriendly. The dog will seek a dark, quiet place to hide; there will be a change in his voice, loss of appetite, and an inability to drink water. As the disease progresses, the dog will become unable to swallow, he will foam at the mouth and drool excess saliva—thus the traditional picture of the mad dog.

Rabies affects dogs in opposite ways. Some dogs become depressed; this is called the dumb form. The lower jaw droops; he drools and makes no noise. The dog quietly awaits death, which will take place in a few days.

In the furious form the dog will roam and bite anything in his way. This, of course, is the way the disease is spread. If you suspect your dog has rabies, he should be confined for ten days, during which time he will die if your suspicions are right.

Since a protective vaccine is not only readily available but mandatory in many communities before a dog can be licensed, there is very little chance that your dog will have this problem. He will get his first shot when he is about six months old, and the vet will tell you when he should get the next one. Depending on the type, the vaccine lasts for one or two years. The tag the vet will give you should be attached to the dog's collar; when you take your pet on a long trip, you should carry a vet's certificate for all inoculations.

Although you can make sure that your dog is not a threat to you because of rabies, there is always a chance that a strange dog that might bite you has not been so protected. If you receive a bite, no chances should be taken. If the dog is rabid and you do not receive immediate treatment, a horrible death is a certainty. First wash the bite out with tincture of green soap, and get the name and address of the dog's owner. Then go to a doctor—not the vet for you.

The dog that bit you should be confined, and if he dies within ten days, his brain should be examined for rabies by a laboratory. Then your doctor will know how to proceed with your treatment.

Temperature is the best indicator of health. Taking it is not difficult. A dog should be rested and quiet before you take his temperature; exercise will produce a higher reading. Use a rectal thermometer with the bulb end covered with petroleum jelly. Raise the dog's tail and insert the thermometer about one-half its length; hold it there about a minute. The average normal temperature for a puppy is 102.5 degrees, and for an adult dog, 101.7 degrees. A temperature of 103 degrees in a puppy means little, but 106 is high and means serious trouble. In an adult dog 103 degrees means an illness is starting, and 103.5 means that you should call the vet.

Ordinary aspirin will provide temporary control of a high fever until you can get to the vet. The dose is one grain of aspirin for every seven pounds of weight, repeated every three hours. Tablets can be crushed and divided; the standard five grain would be right for a thirty-five-pound dog.

The old idea that a hot, dry nose indicates fever and means your dog is sick is just not so. A dog's nose is for smelling; the other end is for temperature taking.

Teething is just as difficult for a pup as it is for a child. There's no set time for the milk teeth to fall out, but the fourteenth week is usually the height of teething. It starts at the age of two months and continues until the pup is about seven months old. The gums get sore, and the whole system is upset. The pup may run a fever and have a little diarrhea. A good hard natural bone or one of the artificial ones will help ease the pain of his gums and help loosen his milk teeth; it will also help the tartar problem in adult dogs. Your dog will be less destructive around the house if you supply him with some good chewing material at this time.

Teeth cause a dog problems. Don't feed him sweets and his teeth won't decay. Tartar is a normal problem; it forms a scale on the dog's teeth, forcing the gums to recede, after which the teeth will become loose and possibly fall out. Removing the tartar is a job for the vet. You can help the situation by scrubbing Fido's teeth. This suggestion usually brings a raised eyebrow, but you should scrub his teeth, using either a child's brush or a rough towel. Scrub the outside of his teeth with an up-and-down motion. This isn't a daily routine, but it should be done every few weeks. His breath will be better, too. Incidentally, while talking about teeth, it's not very sporting of a dog to bite a man. The dog has forty-two teeth, while a man has thirty-two.

FIRST AID

An injured animal may be frightened and confused. Even a normally gentle animal may bite or scratch a person attempting to help it. Therefore, the first thing to keep in mind is to protect yourself. If the animal injures you, you may then be unable to give it assistance. Injured animals often appear dead or in deep shock and unable to move. However, when disturbed they will often use their remaining strength to run away. Therefore, in coming to the aid of an injured animal, take the following steps:

1. Approach the animal slowly and speak to it in a quiet voice.
2. Make a large noose from a leash, belt, string, or strip of cloth, and loop it snugly around the animal's neck.
3. If it appears that the animal may bite, have one person tie a string or bandage around its mouth while another holds the noose.
4. Control bleeding with a pressure bandage.
5. If the animal appears severely injured, cover it with a coat or blanket to keep it warm.
6. Call a veterinarian for further instructions.

To move an injured animal:

1. Lay a coat or blanket on the ground along and under the spine of the animal.
2. Gently roll the animal over on its back onto the blanket.
3. Hold the corners of the blanket and carry it as a stretcher.

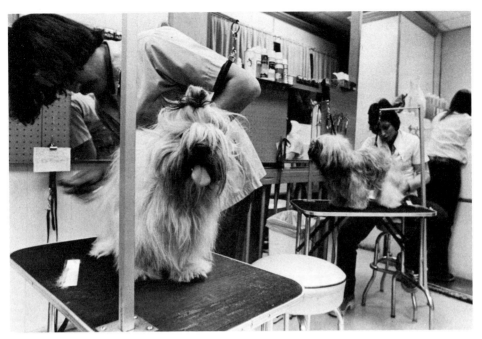

Some dogs are better groomed than most people. Both the dog and the groomer on the left need a trim.

GROOMING YOUR DOG

Tangles and Matting. If a dog's coat is neglected, it can be an awful job to get it back in shape. *Tangles* have to be teased out with a comb. Most likely you'll have to cut the *mats* out completely. But before you resort to that, try cutting the mat into strands parallel to the hair. Hold the fur close to the skin and tease the matting out with a comb. If the scissors have to be used too much, he's going to take on a rather ragged, shabby look. It is an act of love to brush and comb your dog's coat every day, and its healthy shine will amply reward you.

Burrs can be removed from a dog's coat by rubbing mineral oil into the tangle. If long-haired dogs are going to run in brush cover, they should have the hair under their legs trimmed short so they won't pick up burrs. Burrs in the "armpits" will rub until blood is drawn.

Summer haircuts are not a kindness to your dog. His hair insulates him from the heat and protects him from bites of all kinds of pesky insects. Close cuts will expose him to sunburn. Besides, short hair will prick him and itch.

Dandruff is as wrong for your dog as it is for you. It can be caused by parasites, too many baths with caustic soap, or a faulty diet. If Towser has it, seems free of parasites, and you don't suspect the bath problem, try adjusting his diet. Increase the fat by giving him a tablespoon of polyunsaturated oil each day.

Toenails need attention, but owners of city dogs who often walk them on concrete will have less to do than owners who keep them housebound. Cement pavements usually wear the nails off. A good test as to when a dog really needs his nails clipped is to have him walk across a wood floor. If his nails click, they need clipping.

The pup will be easier to handle if he gets used to the clipping at a very young age. It is only natural for him to struggle, but don't scold him—you'll only make the situation worse. Be firm; let him learn that nail clipping is something he is going to have to put up with. A young pup's nails are like needles, and the sooner you start regular care of them the better.

Have a friend help the first few times you trim the puppy's nails. Hold his paw firmly. The guillotine type of nail clipper is best. Put the oval of the clipper over the nail so the blade slides up from the bottom of the nail. It's best to clip a little at a time so that you don't cut into the quick. When you've finished, a few strokes with a file will prevent rough edges from catching on things and splitting the nail.

Tails may get hurt at the tip, especially if your dog sometimes runs in heavy brush in the park or elsewhere. Cut a finger from a leather glove, slip it over the sore tail tip, and fasten it with a generous amount of adhesive tape.

YOUR DOG AND THE LAW

Laws relating to your dog are mostly local. There are so many such laws in all sections of the country that it would take volumes to present them all. If you live in an apartment, be sure to check the fine print of your lease before you bring the pup home. If it excludes dogs, your landlord can force you to get rid of it.

The very young puppy may not need a license for a few weeks, but be sure to find out at what age one is required. You may be sure every city dog must have one; even his country cousin needs a license in most communities.

Leash laws are much more varied. They may be on the book and more or less strictly enforced. One variation is that a dog must be muzzled to roam free. Another, called a nuisance law, allows your dog his freedom until your neighbors complain that he's a pest. Curb your dog if it's the law, or you'll pay the fine. Some localities insist that you clean up after Fido.

If you take your dog to the country for a vacation, remember that a game warden has the legal right to shoot and kill a dog that chases deer. Owners of dogs that have injured or killed livestock are liable for the damages, and certain states allow a farmer to put out poison to kill dogs that harm his animals.

Practically all states have some provisions requiring rabies shots for your dog.

If your dog bites someone, how liable are you? Common law holds that a dog is entitled to bite one person; after that the owner is responsible unless the person bitten is found negligent. A person would be negligent if he trespassed, ignored "Beware of Dog" signs, or teased the dog. Bite cases are the most common cause for damage suits, but dog fights can also bring lawsuits. Local laws will determine responsibility.

Federal law sets rates for transporting dogs across state lines, if you use common carriers. There are also regulations regarding crating, shots, and health certificates.

Cruelty to animals is a criminal action in some states, and laws to protect your dog are extensive. Cropped ears and docked tails are considered forms of cruelty in certain places. You can find out the regulations in your town through the local SPCA, your vet, or the local police.

Barking dogs may not be expected to bite, but in an apartment they may be sufficient grounds for your landlord to bring suit against you, break your lease, and dispossess you. Any dog who barks incessantly, especially at night, is legally regarded as a nuisance.

Laws regarding your treatment of a stray dog that comes to your door are confusing. The law is aimed at the professional dognapper who pretends to have found the precious pet, so, ironically, if you feed a stray, you could find your kindness leading to a police summons. To compound the problem, if you happen to take in a dog for any length of time, you are required to give him food and shelter as long as he stays around.

Insurance companies have planned some protection for you, and for your dog, at home or away. You can obtain insurance coverage for the damage Towser might do in motels or for his hospitalization if he gets hurt.

Some means of *identification* are necessary so that people can identify you as the owner of the dog. After all, in court the dog can't say, "That's my Papa (or Mommy)." Your name, address, and telephone number will do the job. Never put Towser's name on the tag—that's the first thing a dognapper will look for. Have a good photograph of your dog at home so that you will be able to identify him if someone claims that he's their dog.

The National Dog Registry is the best insurance you can buy to protect your dog from dognapping. For a fee of $15 you register your name and address and use your Social Security number as your identification. That number is then tattooed on the dog's inner right hind leg. The fee covers all dogs you will ever own in your lifetime. There is no added charge for more than one dog. Tattooing is painless, only takes a few minutes, and is permanent. The Registry does not do the tattooing; it's done by your vet or through the auspices of kennel clubs or the Humane Society. Most of the medical schools and medical laboratories in the country are cooperating with the Registry and will not buy or use dogs in their experimental work that are tattooed. You can get an application by writing to the National Dog Registry, 227 Stebbins Road, Carmel, New York, 10512.

That's the story. If you have read this far you've undoubtedly learned some new things. Researching this material and putting it into practice has taught me a lot too.

The commands SIT, STAY, and COME are the ball game and are extremely important in the training of a dog. These commands must be obeyed, not only when the dog wants to but whenever they are given—even at a distance from the dog. If you will stick at these commands until the dog learns to obey them immediately, you will be able to teach the dog anything within the realm of his learning.

One of the most important things to remember is, if something does go wrong along the way, don't be so fast to blame the dog . . . look to see what you're doing wrong. Consistency is the name of the game when it comes to training any animal. Second only to that is the balance between reprimand and affection; you are not only the teacher, but you are the friend too. With these things in mind, and properly applied, you are bound to have the best dog in your neighborhood, and a lot of fun besides.

INDEX

HEEL,, 72, 74, 120, 121, 122–123, 128–29, 130
Hepatitis, 174
Hot spot, 172
Housebreaking, 26, 58–61, 115

Identification, 179
Inside turn, 74
Insurance, 179
Intelligence, 93
Irritations, 57

Jumping up, 151

Kennel-Aire, 147

Law, 178–79
Learning, 43, 44, 106–7, 108, 109, 110–14
Leash Law, 178
Leptospirosis, 174
Lice, 171
License, 178
Listless pup, 27
Lock, Jeff, 91

Mange, 171
Mental development, 25, 38–44, 47
Mosquitoes, 171

Nagging, 50
Naming, 46
National Dog Registry, 179
NO, 116

Outside turn, 72
Owner's responsibility, 61–63, 178–79

Parasites, 171
Pecking order, 40
Population, 15, 166
Problem eater, 169
Problems, 142–53
Professional trainer, 68–102, 132–34
Puppy Behavior Test, 27–36

Rabies, 174
Reprimand, 46–48

Restrictions, 57, 58, 126–27
Ringworm, 171
Roscoe B. Jackson Memorial Laboratory, 40, 41, 42, 56

SEARCH command, 157
Selecting the puppy, 24–37
Self-feeding, 168
Sensuous dog, 152
Sex, 23–24, 40
SIT, 76, 77, 78, 79
SIT-STAY, 117, 118–19
Sleeping quarters, 58
Spaying, 166
SPCA, 166
Starting the commands, 65–67, 93–95
Starting the pup, 55
STAY, 80
Street alarm, 158–63
Stress, 38

Tail, 178
Tattooing, 179
Teaching a concept, 100
Teaching role, 45–46
Teeth, 25, 175
Teething, 175
Temperament test, 27–37, 46, 47, 142, 143
Temperature, 175
Throw cans, 146
Ticks, 171
Toenails, 178
Toys, 149
Traffic, 122–23
Trust, 124–25
Turns, 72, 74

Umbilical hernia, 25
Unconscious learning, 44, 106

Veterinarian, 170
Voice, 46, 48–49

Worms, 172
Worrier, 143

ABOUT THE AUTHOR

A native of Pennsylvania, Richard A. Wolters graduated in chemistry and fine arts from Penn State and went into rocket and atomic research. After witnessing four atomic explosions, he saw no future in bombs and turned to art and journalism. Trained in photography by Fritz Goro of *Life*, he has contributed pictures to many national magazines and has been an art director for *Sports Illustrated* and *Business Week*. His effective use of the rapid-sequence camera is shown in many of the photographs in *Home Dog*. All-around sportsman and pioneer in applying modern scientific findings to dog training, Dick Wolters's revolutionary methods are set forth in his highly popular training books, *Gun Dog, Family Dog, Water Dog, Game Dog*, and now *Home Dog*. His historical book, *The Labrador Retriever: The History . . . The People*, was named Best Dog Book of the Year by the Dog Writers Association of America. Dick Wolters is a columnist for *Gun Dog* magazine and has contributed to many other periodicals. He has done dog-training shows on television and has conducted many training seminars. He also enjoys ballooning and flying sailplanes, in which he holds the most advanced ratings.